THE PRAIRIE
WATER
GARDEN

Paul Harris & Terry Warke

Red Deer College Press

The Publishers
Red Deer Press
813 MacKimmie Library Tower
2500 University Drive N.W.
Calgary Alberta Canada T2N 1N4

Credits
Cover design by Boldface Technology.
Text design by Dennis Johnson.
Printed and bound in Canada by Friesens for Red Deer Press.

Acknowledgments
Financial support provided by the Alberta Foundation for the Arts, a beneficiary of the Lottery Fund of the Government of Alberta, and by the Canada Council, the Department of Canadian Heritage and Red Deer College.

COMMITTED TO THE DEVELOPMENT OF CULTURE AND THE ARTS

THE CANADA COUNCIL FOR THE ARTS SINCE 1957 | LE CONSEIL DES ARTS DU CANADA DEPUIS 1957

Canadian Cataloguing in Publication Data
Harris, Paul, 1962–
The prairie water garden
(Prairie garden books)
ISBN 0-88995-175-6
1. Water gardens—Prairie provinces. I. Warke, Terry, 1958– II. Title. III. Series.
SB423.H37 1998   635.9'674'09712   C98-910246-7

5 4 3 2

To all of our friends, past,
present and yet to be.

Acknowledgments

We wish to offer our sincere appreciation to the many friends and family members who supported us throughout our first book project. Without them this would never have been possible.

Thanks also to Terry's mother, Doris Warke; to Margaret Day and Garry Krausher, trusted friends for volunteering to tend our shop for so many days while we wrestled with the contents of this book; a profound thank-you to our ever-present and dedicated shop manager, Betty Hattori, who fielded messages, proofread and typed, listened to us moan about our too-busy lives and generally did triple duty during this whole project. Thanks as well to Virginia Hays for permission to photograph the construction of her pond, shown on pages 44 and 45, and to Keith and Delores Fox of Delky Greenhouses for permission to photograph the gardens on pages 32 and 106.

Special thanks also to Jan and Heinjo Lahring of Bearberry Creek Water Gardens, who allowed us to visit often for advice, for pictures and for their expertise. A great many of the photographs in this book are courtesy of Jan and Heinjo. Thanks also are extended to Toko Garden Design for permission to photograph designs on pages 12, 24, 38 and 46, and to The Landscape Artist for designs on pages 14, 22 and 27.

Of course, thanks to all of the avid water gardeners who let us come into their yards to take pictures of the great things they have created and grown.

No acknowledgment would be complete without a sincere thanks to our new friends Dennis Johnson and Carolyn Dearden of Red Deer College Press, who put up with our busy schedules and yet found the time to work with us through all of the challenges of this book.

Last, but not least, we thank our families, who have encouraged us to believe in ourselves and who have supported us every step of the way.

—PH & TW

Contents

THE PRAIRIE
WATER
GARDEN

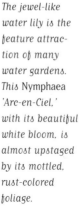

The Magic of Water Gardens

The jewel-like water lily is the feature attraction of many water gardens. This Nymphaea 'Arc-en-Ciel,' with its beautiful white bloom, is almost upstaged by its mottled, rust-colored foliage.

WATER IS THE SOURCE OF LIFE, both practically and symbolically, and perhaps that is its fascination for the gardener. The presence of water is something we take deep, almost unconscious pleasure and comfort in. In motion, water can provide refreshing coolness in the heat of a prairie summer day and can be the source of soothing sounds that screen out the unwanted distractions of urban life. At rest, water can be a mirror, multiplying what surrounds it and doubling our delight in favorite blooms. Sunlight shining through a fountain can create a rainbow, and night deepens the mystery of water, especially if illuminated by the moon, subtle, indirect electrical lighting or even floating candles.

Whatever size your gardening space, you and even the creatures

 9

Brilliantly colored potted annuals frame this miniature lion head fountain and demonstrate what can be achieved even in small spaces.

around you can benefit from the sights and sounds of water. Water gardens have a magic that attracts visitors of all descriptions. Some—like snails, toads and salamanders—come to stay. Others, like birds and squirrels, come to drink, bathe and play. People come because water draws them like a spell.

Any combination of a water container and water-loving plants can be a water garden. Maybe your imagination runs to a large, still pond with water lilies swaying gently on the surface and a fountain or

waterfall splashing in the background. Perhaps your fancy turns to a gently flowing stream crossed by stepping stones or a bridge. If space is limited perhaps your water garden will be a miniature lion-head fountain on your balcony or a container holding a single splendid water lily in full bloom on a deck. Large or small, elaborate or simple, water features will make your garden more beautiful, more interesting and more vibrant.

Some believe that water gardens on the prairies are interesting to

*Even a single
splendid lily,
such as this
Nymphaea
'Fabiola,' adds
ambiance to the
garden setting.*

enjoy only in someone else's yard because they are too difficult to build and maintain. Thankfully, that's a myth. With careful study, planning and a little work you too can enjoy the beauty of a water garden without a lot of maintenance.

Throughout this book we'll share step-by-step design, construction, planting and maintenance ideas for water features sure to please any taste. Illustrations and photographs supply additional guidance and inspiration.

Chapter 1, "Designing Water Gar-dens," helps you identify practical issues that affect the style, size and placement of a water feature in your garden. From there we turn to aesthetic issues and explore design principles and elements. You will learn how various design elements interact and affect your overall garden design. Then we'll explore the many different types of water features, from containers placed on decks and garden paths, to formal structures that tie into your existing architecture, to designs that appear as if created by nature itself. You

Solid stone and supple water beautifully showcase N. 'Attraction' lilies in this garden pond.

will be guided through the process of taking an inventory of your existing landscape design, assessing your additional needs and determining the best size, placement and style of your water garden. A checklist is provided to guide you through the design stage.

Chapter 2, "Constructing Water Gardens," leads you through the process that brings your design to life in your landscape. You will examine the many types of construction materials, their potential costs and look at options for creating attractive pond edges. Illustrations and easy-to-follow instructions will guide you through the steps of excavating a pool, installing a pond liner and working with pond edges. You also will learn about the preparation of bog soil.

The pond allows you to cultivate a variety of interesting water-loving species, while the edges lend themselves to moisture-loving bog and rockery or alpine plants. Chapter 3, "Planting Water Gardens," contains a comprehensive list of plant material, complete with flower description, height, spread, hardiness zone, bloom time and planting conditions. The potting and planting of marginal, emergent, submerged, deepwater and free-floating plants in the five zones of your pond are described and illustrated.

With your water feature constructed and appropriate plants in place, the maintenance cycle begins. Chapter 4, "Maintaining Water Gardens," takes you season by season through establishing and maintaining the proper ecological balance in your pond and caring for the plant life it supports. You'll also learn about overwintering delicate species like water lilies.

Chapter 5, "Stocking Fish and Attracting Wildlife," is devoted to attracting and maintaining animal life in and around your pond. Fish, amphibians, mammals and birds have special needs that you will need to consider if they are to accept your invitation to make your pond their home.

The moment you fill your new feature with water, you can start to enjoy its beauty and ambiance. You can expect it to become a refuge for family, friends and wildlife that connects you to a tradition stretching back thirty-five hundred years to ancient Egyptian gardeners who discovered that irrigation channels could be not only practical but aesthetic. In the water garden, time is measured by the rhythms of nature. Jewel-like water lilies might mingle with native prairie grasses and cattails. Fish might move contentedly beneath the surface while iridescent dragonflies hover above. At one end of the pond, water might cascade through a series of basins. With such a garden scene it's easy to understand why gardening with water is one of the fastest growing trends in garden design.

Over the years we've helped many people create water garden getaways, and we've seen firsthand the pleasure they bring. We hope this book inspires you to look at your landscape anew, to get some prairie dirt under your fingernails and to begin creating.

CHAPTER 1

Designing Water Gardens

With some study and careful planning, designing such a backyard paradise is well within the reach of the water garden enthusiast.

WATER IS PERHAPS THE MOST versatile and adaptable element you can introduce into your garden. Water is a perfect addition to any setting, informal or formal, and on any scale, from a small container on an apartment balcony to a substantial recreational pond on an acreage. Whatever its application, water is the melody in your garden symphony. Like melodies, water creates a mood that can be light and airy, dark and mysterious, or anything in between. You are your garden's composer and conductor, and whatever variety of water feature you design, it should reflect your personality and harmonize with the whole of your garden.

If you are lucky enough to have a natural slope in your yard, you might, for instance, consider a cascading waterfall that blends with a

15

This backyard oasis with its rustic canopy and twig furniture is enhanced by a small, raised reflecting pool.

hillside rock garden, or a meandering stream that encourages you to relax and enjoy the feeling that you have been transported to a meadow far away from the hustle and bustle of urban life.

If your landscape is without a natural slope, you might consider a still pond, where reflections of clouds shift among floating water lilies. The soothing sights and sounds of moving water can be achieved through the addition of a fountain. Can you think of better way to add all features of nature to your garden symphony?

Confined spaces such as apartment balconies can also enjoy the melody of moving water. A single note in your symphony could be a one-piece Victorian wall fountain reproduction featuring a gargoyle or animal mask, or a waterproof polyurethane model finished to look like old marble. Installation takes no more than an hour.

Miniature water gardens can be planted in just about any watertight container: an oriental ginger pot, a duck-egg container, a ceramic or porcelain basin, an urn, half of a wooden whiskey barrel or a decorative plastic planter. Even a small container with a single lily can strike a dramatic chord on a balcony, patio or deck.

With the image of your perfect water garden in mind, it may be tempting to rush into the garden, shovel in hand, and begin excavating. But restrain your enthusiasm and focus first on assessing your needs, analyzing your landscape and mastering some basic principles of design. Working sequentially through the steps in the design process will ensure that your water feature meets your needs and harmonizes with your existing garden setting. After all, permanent water features are just that, and you don't

want to construct a large waterfall near your bedroom window only to discover that you can't sleep through the sound, just as you don't want to complete a substantial pond only to find that you have no comfortable access to utilities to refill it or operate your pump.

STEP 1
Assessing Personal Needs

Decide what role you want water to play in your overall garden design and what ambiance you want to create. Do you want, for example, a dramatic focal piece or a quiet, hidden oasis in the garden? Will a small, portable water fountain or container suffice, or will your project require major excava-

tion? If moving water will be a feature, will it be an attention-grabbing cascade or a barely audible trickle?

Because water features can easily dominate the garden setting you should consider how far you want the ambiance to extend into your outdoor and even indoor living spaces. What areas in your home and garden do you occupy most frequently? Do you desire a view of your water feature from inside your house? Or do you want it tucked into a quiet alcove, where it will provide a sense of discovery?

To gather ideas for your own water feature, carefully study books, magazines, television programs, computer assisted garden

TOP: A formal water feature is well suited to formal surroundings.

BOTTOM: An informal setting is perfect for an informal pond with natural-looking falls.

Bordered by a stone stairway and path, this formal, semicircular pond is well framed by manicured turf and flower beds. The balanced plantings in and around the pond reinforce the formal approach. The pond's formality is softened by the use of natural stone.

design programs, and existing public and private gardens. Visit garden centers to learn how the atmosphere you desire can be achieved. Become a member of a garden club or society and seek advice from gardeners who've constructed water features. Generally, you'll find them the most congenial of hosts and more than willing to share their experience. Collect pictures and sketch ideas.

STEP 2
Analyzing Style

Your water garden feature—large or small, prominent or secluded, near an existing structure or standing alone—should blend seamlessly into your present landscape. Survey your garden to determine its general *style*. Is it *formal*, with geometric circles or angles reflecting the architecture of adjacent buildings? Or is it *informal*, with irregular shapes that could have been contoured by nature? Is it a combination of formal and informal?

A symmetrically shaped formal water garden is ideally suited to settings where walkways and flower beds are geometric, manicured and in tune with existing architecture such as houses, garages, decks, potting sheds and gazebos. The pool may be constructed of cement or a preformed rigid pond shell and may be bordered by wooden decks, stone pathways or poured concrete. Because of the materials typically used in formal pond construction, a smooth natural transition to the rest of the garden is not easily attainable. But people may approach the water garden to its very edge to observe plants and animals, something that can't often be done in nature. Formal ponds have the advantage of being a little easier to construct than informal ponds, but the materials may be

more expensive and may, especially in case of concrete, require professional installation.

An informal water garden is best suited to landscapes with softly curved flower beds and meandering pathways. Water gardens in such casual settings should appear as if they've always been part of the garden. Informal ponds also tend to be more adaptable to a range of settings, but they may require more thorough and thoughtful planning. Generally, the effect is easier to accomplish if the pond is placed some distance from existing architecture. Informal ponds are typically more difficult to construct, but the extra effort pays off with fluid transitions between water and land supplied by bog and other moisture-loving plants.

Nothing precludes mixing formal and informal styles in your landscape. You can, for instance, place an informal pond near your home provided that you establish a transitional zone between the formality of the architecture and the informality of the pond. Oriental themes accomplish the task admirably. Their informal ponds and streams contrast formal structures such as walkways, bridges and viewing areas that appear as if constructed later to take advantage of nature's beauty.

Your water garden design may additionally reflect an existing dominant garden *theme* that elaborates a basic formal or informal style. It may exhibit the simplicity, tranquillity and grace of a Japanese theme. Relying strongly on symbolism, it uses plant material, sand, gravel aggregates and sculptured stone to encourage relaxation and inspire meditation. Typical English or Victorian compositions use clean, straight lines and geometric

This informal garden mimics nature in its shape, irregular stone border and sheer abundance of vegetation.

The structures and walkways of this Japanese garden appear as if designed to take advantage of a natural water setting.

forms. It's a colorful, often eclectic mix of perennials, including topiaries. Early American themes are symmetrical and practical. Typically surrounded by a hedge, they favor herbs, vegetables and other functional plants. The popular New American garden composition is more asymmetrical and stresses a four-season approach. A mix of perennial and woody plants provides a succession of visually stimulating scenery. Contemporary themes emphasize simple and uncluttered environments with single-specimen plantings. They are ideally suited to people who don't enjoy high-maintenance gardening but need some elegance in the landscape. Your water garden design may complement or contrast the theme that dominates your garden, but it must harmonize with the general style, whether formal or informal.

STEP 3

Determining Size

A water garden must be in scale with the property itself and with intended plant material. A small oasis hidden in the corner of a large city garden will be a delight to visitors, but a tiny pond placed in a vast acreage lawn will look like a misplaced puddle. A country acreage with clay subsoil and natural springs is better suited to a pond large enough for recreational activities such as swimming. Small lily ponds and container gardens are better choices for a tiny urban lot.

Bigger ponds will have the advantage of less maintenance. A greater volume of water will maintain more consistent temperature and is easier to keep ecologically balanced. Larger ponds tend to be more algae free, their fish and plants less prone to disease and their filters less in need of frequent cleaning. Larger

ponds also can assimilate a certain amount of methane released from decomposing leaves that sink to the bottom in the autumn. If the pond has not only size but considerable depth, it may not freeze solid in winter, so certain plants and fish can be overwintered in the pond with a minimum of maintenance.

Smaller ponds will require more frequent attention, but they can still host a pleasing variety of aquatic life. For example, every square yard (.8 square meters) of water surface can typically accommodate one large water lily, two bunches of grasses, two goldfish or smaller koi, and a dozen ramshorn snails in a pond approximately 3' (91 cm) deep.

TOP: *The theme of this Japanese-style alcove is enhanced by a traditional shishi odoshi spilling water into the pool. In a moment, it will return to the vertical position to fill again, making a hollow clack as the bottom strikes the small rock. The shishi odoshi was originally intended to scare deer away from the garden.*

BOTTOM: *The reflective qualities of water can be used to make a small pond appear larger.*

This New American theme garden steps down through irregularly spaced stone terraces to a small stream. Plantings of annuals, perennials, grasses and shrubs provide four-season interest.

Step 4

Determining Placement

Your water feature will need to be placed in your garden setting with consideration for the safety of children and visitors, bylaws of your city or municipality, accessibility to utilities and the rest of the yard, ease of maintenance, aquatic plants you desire and wildlife you hope to attract.

Your pond is for enjoyment, not constant worry. Choose a location that is safe. If children frequent your garden, you may have to fence your yard or the pond area to protect them. Many cities, for instance, consider ponds deeper than 24" (61 cm) as swimming pools and have strict guidelines regarding placement and safety fencing. Check restrictions with local authorities before you make final decisions on the size and placement of your pond.

Safety fencing doesn't have to mean chain-link. Bamboo or lattice screens, retaining walls and hedges are just a few options to consider. Even if a traditional fence is required there are many types of plants that can transform a potentially ugly structure into a natural part of your garden. Consider growing such plants as Virginia creeper (*Parthenocissus quinquefolia*), clematis (*Clematis* spp.), sweet peas (*Lathyrus odoratus*), hollyhocks (*Althaea rosea*) or other tall species to conceal an unsightly fence and provide an interesting backdrop for your water garden.

Other practical issues to consider include the location of utilities and the accessibility of the site. Access to water and electricity will be required to operate and maintain and your water feature. Neither water nor electricity is difficult to bring to your pond site, but the greater the distance, the more expensive and complicated construction will be. Excavating a pond also can damage utility lines, so always have authorities mark locations before committing to a final location.

You also must consider how accessible your site will be for equipment needed in construction. A large, deep pond may require earth-moving and hauling equipment. As a general rule a small skid steer loader (in lay terms, a Bobcat) requires a clear path approximately 6' (1.8 m) wide and a turning area of about 15' (4.5 m). If you're determined to construct in a location that isn't convenient for power equipment, you may have to consider scaling back the size of your pond or digging it by hand.

Take into account future projects around your home and garden. After your water feature is constructed and the plant material has matured, can you, if needed, maneuver a loader or truck past your beautiful work without destroying it? In the enthusiasm of the creative moment you may not wish to contemplate future projects, but you must, especially if you have a growing family whose needs will change over time.

The location of the water feature will affect the frequency and extent of maintenance. A pond placed too near large deciduous trees will become filled with leaves in the autumn. They will discolor the water, reduce oxygen levels necessary for thriving pond life, potentially clog overflow channels or pumps and generally be a nuisance.

Placement will affect the plants you can to grow in and around the water garden. Is the proposed site in the sun or shade? Is it well sheltered from prevailing winds that may disturb the water's surface? Most water lilies, for example, prefer still water and require a minimum of six hours of sunlight to reward you with beautiful blooms. Ideally, your pond should be located where the shadows of tall trees

A stream appears as if constructed by nature. Asymmetrical plantings of deciduous trees give way at streamside to junipers and low-growing bushes, and then to boulders and smooth stones— all in keeping with the scale of the water feature.

The size of the pond in this Japanese-inspired garden is perfectly in keeping with the scale of the landscape, and its placement allows easy viewing from the deck. Masses of shrubbery and boulders screen the fence in the background.

and shrubs do not fall on the pond during the heat of the afternoon.

A final practical consideration is locating your pond where wildlife will feel welcome. Microscopic water life and aquatic insects could care less where the pond is and birds may be relatively daring, but amphibians and small mammals prefer a location that is some distance from your home.

Having determined one or more suitable locations for your pond, lay an old mirror on the ground at the proposed sites to check the water feature's reflective qualities. Stand back and examine the reflection of the various garden elements that already exist. Some you will want; others you will block with plantings in and around the pond. The mirror also will give you some idea of the view from the decks, windows and other living spaces from which your pond will be visible.

If considering the placement of a moving water feature, you will need to gauge the sound level. For a cascading waterfall, set a garden hose to run into a bucket from a height of 3–4' (91–122 cm) and stand back to judge the sound from various distances. The sound should not interfere with conversation or sleep. The more audible your feature, the farther you will want to place it from your home and conversation areas in the garden. Unless you have the space for grand water features, this may be one of those times when bigger is not better. Alternately, you will have to mute the sound by constructing your waterfall so that it flows gently over small pebbles and smooth stones.

Whether prominent or secluded, stimulating or relaxing, a pond has intrinsic beauty. The water's surface will mirror the nature around it, doubling your efforts and claiming even the sky as part of the garden scene. The rippling quality of water will bring movement to the garden and will be a source of relaxation. Water gently splashing over rocks into a pond inspires listeners to recall time spent enjoying nature, perhaps hiking in the mountains and camping in a meadow.

STEP 5
Determining Budget

Your pond can be as large and elaborate as imagination and location allow, but you inevitably must turn your attention to cost. If your plans exceed your budget, consider constructing your water feature in stages over two or even three seasons. As with home furnishings, sometimes it's better to purchase quality pieces one at a time than to settle immediately for a complete ensemble that will be less satisfying over the long term. Extending construction over a few seasons will, however, make the initial design process critical. Invest in the first season on design and construction, and delay purchase of fountains, pumps and more expensive plants until your budget permits.

STEP 6
Assessing Design Elements

With the general issues of style, size and placement resolved, you can turn your attention to designing the specifics of the water feature itself. To do this you need to master a few basic design concepts that at their most fundamental include points, lines, planes, shapes and forms and the two attributes of these, namely color and texture.

POINTS

Technically, a *point* is a one-dimensional element without breadth, width or height, but we gardener's take a less literal definition and view it as a single occurrence of something. A point can be, for example, an urn on a deck, a tree in the yard or a single stunning water lily in an oriental ceramic basin.

LINES

A *line* is an extension of one point in one dimension to another point or series of points. For

The straight lines and hard angles of this house and rectangular pond are softened by curved pathways and flower beds.

*Straight lines
and flat planes
are softened by
the fine textures
of marginal
plantings and by
cascading vines
over the arbor.*

instance, a row of stepping stones weaving across a pond are individual points that collectively form a line. You will discover many important lines in your landscape. Natural lines exist in tree trunks, edges of plantings and even the skyline or horizon. Artificial lines can be found in fences, roads and other boundaries. The lines defining the edges of your water garden and the various shapes it contains should complement the existing lines in your garden, whether straight or curved. It's often helpful to sketch an overhead view of your landscape roughly to scale to help you visualize the most harmonious extension of existing lines.

However, the lines of your garden are seldom viewed from overhead, but rather from garden paths, windows, a deck or favorite bench. These so-called *sight line* views are visual pathways, allowing you the most pleasing perspectives and unobstructed enjoyment of your water garden from your favorite vantages.

PLANES

A *plane* adds one more dimension to a line. Planes are flat and include elements such as the side of a building, the surface of your pond and the lawn between your water feature and other plantings.

SHAPES

The edges of a plane outline a *shape*. Shapes range from simple to complex and from the irregular organic to the regular geometric. A garden mixing organic and geometric shapes indiscriminately tends to create tension and visual confusion in the viewer. An informal pond, for example, should not directly border your house, garage or any other geometric structure. Thoughtful garden design results in a consistency of shape or gradual transitions from predominately natural to geometric shapes. With careful planning you can integrate an informal water feature into a largely geometric landscape and produce beautiful results.

FORMS

Form is the three-dimensional counterpart of shape. For instance, a ball and a cube are the counterparts of a circle and a square. Form is very important to garden design because it takes on the attributes of color and texture.

All color is composed of the three *primary colors:* red, yellow and blue. Imagine these as the three points of a triangle, and then draw a circle around the points. This circle will represent the *color wheel.* Combining the primary colors two at a time will produce *secondary colors,* which are represented as a second triangle with its points falling directly between those of the first. These colors are orange, purple and green.

Adding two more triangles creates *tertiary colors.* Between the primary color yellow and the secondary color green, for instance, is the tertiary color yellow-green. The five other tertiary colors are green-blue, blue-purple, purple-red, red-orange and orange-yellow. Adding more points to the color wheel produces still subtler variations. Note,

however, that naming colors after the primaries and secondaries is arbitrary and subjective at best.

To use the design element of color effectively in the garden, you need to convert the color wheel into a stack of wheels. The basic color wheel will be at the center. The wheels above will have progressively more white added until the top of the stack contains pale pastels and off-whites. The wheels below will have black added sequentially until the bottom wheel represents colors as they are seen at night.

The natural-stone stairway from the viewing terrace follows a gently flowing S-shape down to the reflecting pool. Evergreens screen the rigid geometry of the fence and houses.

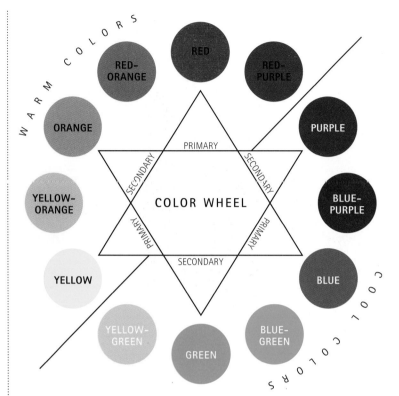

Adding white or black to a color changes its *luminosity*. The colors on any single wheel have the same intensity, so none dominates the others. However, the same colors from different wheels will have different intensities, so one color will be dominant.

Color elicits emotional response and thus enhances atmosphere or mood in the garden. Red, orange and yellow are experienced as warm and stimulating; purple, blue and green are cool and serene. Adding white to any color changes the mood to airy, optimistic and romantic. Adding black transforms the mood to subdued, meditative and regal. Increasing the luminosity of red to make pastel pink, for instance, increases the suggestion of romance. Conversely, decreasing the luminosity to produce a deep burgundy suggests a contemplative mood. Color combinations should be chosen to reinforce the ambiance you desire. What atmosphere do you want your garden to project? Energizing or calming? Stately or romantic? Joyful or contemplative? It's up to you.

Complementary color combinations appear next to each other on the color wheel. For example, red and orange are complementary, a principle that holds true no matter what the luminosity of the colors. *Analogous color schemes* use any

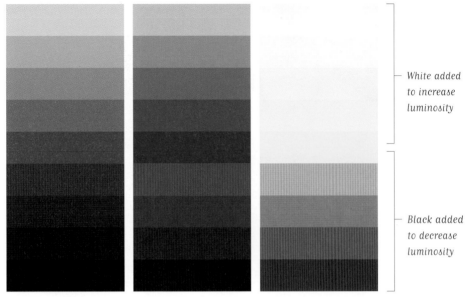

White added
to increase
luminosity

Black added
to decrease
luminosity

three adjacent colors such as blue, blue-green and green. *Contrasting colors* appear opposite each other on the color wheel. Vibrant holiday colors such as the red and green of Christmas or the purple and yellow of Easter are contrasting. *Monochromatic color schemes* use various luminosities of single colors, such as pink, red and maroon.

A warm harmonious array of analogous colors in the water garden can be created through plantings of water lilies such as the garnet red blooms of *N.* 'Attraction,' the canary yellow of *N.* 'Chromatella' and the apricot yellow of *N.* 'Comanche.' Together they create a stunning focal point on the pond's surface.

A bold display of contrasting colors could involve plantings of bright blue water iris (*Iris laevigata*) in combination with yellow water iris (*Iris pseudacorus*).

A subtle monochromatic scheme might include several deep pink dwarf water lilies such as *Nymphaea pygmaea* var. 'Rubra' set among a few soft pink lilies such as *Nymphaea odorata* var. *rosea* and one or two pure white lilies such as *Nymphaea* 'Virginalis.'

Color schemes should include not just flowers but foliage and stems. Ideally, you want to orchestrate a succession of harmonious color combinations from the earliest emergence of spring foliage through the blooming periods of summer and perhaps even into the retreating colors of autumn.

Color establishes not only ambiance in the garden, but also creates the illusion of enlarged or reduced space. Red, orange and yellow appear closer to viewers and make a space look smaller. Purple, blue and green recede and make a

LEFT: Plants with contrasting colors add visual interest to this garden scene.

RIGHT: The coarse texture of large water-lily leaves in the background gives way to the medium texture of water hyacinth (Eichhornia crassipes) and then to the fine texture of common mare's-tail (Hippuris vulgaris) in the foreground.

space look larger. Luminosity also can create the illusion of increased or diminished space. The greater the luminosity of a color (the more white added), the more it will reflect sunlight, brighten the space and make it appear larger. The opposite is true of colors with less luminosity.

Plant *texture* ranks second in importance in evoking the mood of your garden scene. Gardeners refer to texture's visual character as fine versus coarse, smooth versus rough, light versus heavy or sparse versus dense. A plant's texture is best revealed at a distance. If details are hard to determine, its texture is fine; if they are easily visible, its texture is coarse. For example, the soft whorled leaves of parrot's feather *(Myriophyllum aquaticum)* are fine. The straplike floating leaves of water Hawthorne *(Aponogeton distachyus)* are coarse. Like color, texture can create the illusion of space. Fine textures appear to recede, producing a sense of depth. Coarse textures leap to the eye, seeming closer.

Combining textures creates interest in the water garden. Some designers advocate blending textures gradually from one to the other, but highly contrasting elements immediately adjacent to each other can make a very bold design statement. Texture also can be used to direct the eye through the water garden scene. Coarse textures can be fully appreciated at a distance, but finer textures invite closer inspection.

STEP 7
Designing the Water Garden

The basic elements of point, line, plane, shape and form are the building blocks of design, but they do not in themselves ensure that your final garden composition will be aesthetically pleasing. To achieve this they need to be governed by design principles that have evolved over time and through the experience of many garden designers. Shapes, forms, colors and textures must be artfully organized into compositions that satisfy intrinsic notions of beauty. The following design considerations should govern your selection of construction and plant materials

and their arrangement in the water garden. Your goal is to create a garden scene with an overall sense of harmony, which is achieved through artfully balanced combinations of color, texture and form.

DOMINANCE

Dominance makes one element or group of elements more prominent than others. For example, brightly colored flowers or foliage draw more attention than subdued hues. Coarse textures dominate fine textures. The water garden itself may be a dominant feature or may be blended more subtly into existing garden areas. To create a proper focal point within the water garden, something needs to have dominance, whether it is a single plant or a group of plants, an urn or piece of statuary, a waterfall or fountain.

UNITY

Unity is the harmonious relationship among the various landscape elements of your garden. Although you may have several different themes running throughout, they

need to appear naturally connected. The elements must look as if they belong together and contribute to a sense of oneness within the design. Unity is achieved through the thoughtful manipulation of point, line, shape, and form and its attributes of color and texture. For example, a single flowing curve running through the entire garden can link thematically different garden areas into a unified composition. This unifying curve can be established through planting-bed shapes or through prominent pottery,

Top: A dramatic focal point can be created by planting an area in the center of the pond. The pond liner runs beneath the island, with boulders and bog soil forming a planting bed for interesting marginals.

Bottom: A classically inspired statue and rugged stone fence are the dominant features of this setting.

This lovely garden composition is unified by the stone borders that step naturally down from raised flower beds to become the edge of the pond. The consistently curved shapes and the arrangement of plants and construction materials add a strong sense of rhythm and unity to the overall design.

planters or garden statuary placed at strategic points. These focal points will have the same effect of accenting and unifying the whole.

The grouping of like forms, colors and textures also creates immediate unity. For example, a Japanese archway situated at the entrance to each section of the garden, a single type of stone placed at every focal point, or similar walkway materials throughout the garden will unify your design.

One of the easiest ways to integrate your water garden harmoniously is to work with an overall style, whether formal or informal, or an overall theme such as Japanese, Victorian or New American. For example, an ornate, classically detailed concrete fountain will not harmonize with an otherwise natural setting. To achieve harmony among these discordant styles, transition zones must be developed.

A small area of manicured lawn around a classical fountain could gradually give way to less geometric shapes to establish a buffer between the formal and the informal.

BALANCE

Every landscape element—whether organic or manufactured—occupies a physical space that is its mass. The principle of *balance* controls the even distribution of mass across a central axis. We recognize balance as a kind of visual weight.

Symmetrical balance is achieved when the arrangement of materials on one side of a central axis is mirrored on the other. Asymmetrical balance is accomplished when a mass of one size is balanced by a greater number of objects of a smaller mass. In a formally styled water garden, elements are distributed symmetrically in keeping with the geometric form of the pool. In an informal garden, components are grouped asymmetrically to reflect the free-form shape of the pond.

RHYTHM

Rhythm is a repeated accent that provides a sense of continuity in the garden. Repeated points, lines, shapes and forms create a visual rhythm that moves the eye smoothly through the garden scene. Color and texture are especially important to creating a sense of rhythm. Without rhythm the water garden will appear cluttered and discordant, and will have too many focal points to establish a sense of unity. On the other hand, too much repetition will create monotony.

In the formally styled water garden, rhythm will be very uniform. This could be achieved in a rectangular pond by arranging similar plantings in each of the four corners. This uniformity of rhythm could extend to paving stones of similar size and color used to edge the pond. In the informally styled water garden the repetition of accents will appear more random, but they will nevertheless create a sense of balance. Several small stands of dwarf cattails (*Typha minima*), for example, grouped against a background of massed marsh reed grass (*Calamagrostis canadensis*) will create a strong sense of rhythm.

Today, as more and more gardeners strive to produce natural effects

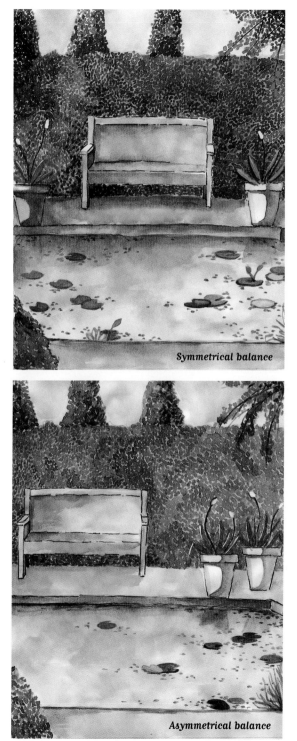

Symmetrical balance

Asymmetrical balance

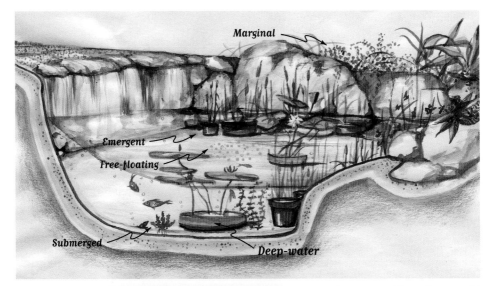

Marginal

Emergent

Free-floating

Submerged

Deep-water

Top: Marginal, emergent, submerged, free-floating and deep-water plants can all find homes in a well-designed water garden.

Bottom: This formal garden setting, with its circular fountain and gravel walkway, is symmetrically balanced with even plantings on either side and a bench perfectly centered on the walkway.

in the garden, the formal style is less favored. Nevertheless, repetition in your garden is still important to its overall unity, balance and rhythm.

CONTRAST

Contrast creates variety and interest through the harmonious combining of different shapes, col-

ors and textures. After all, it would be a dull garden that had only one type of plant material in one color. Contrast provides points of focus in the water garden design, but it's clearly important not to exaggerate contrast to the point of chaos. Interesting contrasts in the water garden can easily be created through the many different shapes, textures and colors of plant material.

STEP 8
Creating a Working Drawing

Armed with the clear knowledge of your personal priorities, your existing landscape and the rudiments of garden design, you are ready to commit your ideas to paper. Using graph paper, translate your ideas into a bird's-eye plan of your water feature in its location. Using colored pencils, plot the position of plant and construction materials. If your water feature

A strong sense of rhythm is created by this trio of simple wooden containers with their upright forms of pencil cattails (Typha angustifolia), irises (Iris spp.) and white rush (Scirpus tabernaemontani 'Albescens').

LEFT: Repetition, contrasting textures and open spaces draw visitors into and through the landscape as the eye follows a natural S-shaped path.

RIGHT: The feathery astilbe spp. contrast the coarse, broad leaves of hosta spp. to bring additional interest to the cast-concrete birdbath, which is the dominant feature of this shady nook.

contains a change in elevation, it may be necessary to sketch an elevation plan. Experiment with shape, color and texture until the design satisfies the fundamentals of dominance, unity, balance, rhythm and contrast. After all, you don't want to discover that your heavy stone waterfall does not harmonize with the water garden scene after the labor of construction is complete.

Finally, don't be shy about experimenting with various designs before settling upon the one that best suits you and your garden. And even then, it may take several seasons of trial and error to achieve the final mood desired. Remember, every garden is a work in progress and a place to make discoveries.

Repeated shapes in the landscape elements and construction materials produce unity in this detailed sketch.

The following checklist will help you take an inventory of your landscape, determine its present style or theme, and decide on the ideal style of water feature for your garden. Work through the list consistently and deliberately to ensure that you take account of every factor that will influence your final water garden design.

Designing Water Gardens Checklist

Ambiance desired:
- ❏ Dramatic focal point?
- ❏ Quiet oasis?
- ❏ Still water?
- ❏ Moving water (fountain, waterfall or stream)?

Survey of existing garden:
- ❏ Formal (geometric shapes)?
- ❏ Informal (natural shapes)?
- ❏ Dominant theme (Victorian, Japanese, Early American, New American, Contemporary)?

Water garden style:
- ❏ Formal (geometric shapes)?
- ❏ Informal (natural shapes)?
- ❏ Dominant theme desired (Victorian, Japanese, Early American, New American, Contemporary)?

Water garden size:
- ❏ Large earth pond?
- ❏ Small pool?
- ❏ Container?
- ❏ Moving water feature?

Water garden placement:
- ❏ Safety of children and visitors considered?
- ❏ Municipal or civic bylaws checked?
- ❏ Water, telephone, natural gas, electrical or other utility lines located?
- ❏ Water and electricity accessible?
- ❏ Site accessible to construction and maintenance equipment now and in the future?

- ❏ Site away from large deciduous trees?
- ❏ Site receives adequate sunlight for aquatic plants?
- ❏ Site suitable to attracting wildlife, if desired?
- ❏ Site's reflective qualities tested?
- ❏ Moving-water sound levels tested?
- ❏ Views from favorite living spaces considered?

Water garden budget:
- ❏ Quotes received for construction materials (liners, edging, pumps, hoses, filters, biofilters, lights, fountains)?
- ❏ Quotes received for electrical installation (if required)?
- ❏ Quotes received for equipment rental (if required)?
- ❏ Quotes received for labor costs (if required)?
- ❏ Quotes received for plant materials?
- ❏ Quotes received for ornaments (birdhouses, statuary)?
- ❏ Project to be completed in one season?
- ❏ Project to be amortized over several seasons?

Designing the water garden:
- ❏ Color and texture schemes determined?
- ❏ Number and variety of plants determined?
- ❏ Planting strategies determined?
- ❏ Bird's-eye and elevation plans sketched to scale?

CHAPTER 2

Constructing Water Gardens

ALL WATER GARDENS MUST HOLD water and be deep enough to support aquatic plant and perhaps animal life, but after that they can be constructed from a broad range of materials in every conceivable size and shape. Your ideal water garden may be as simple as a container placed on a deck or dug into the soil, or as complex as a series of ponds linked by streams and waterfalls. Smaller, more portable container gardens and precast fountains require relatively little labor to install. Larger ponds, however, necessitate careful excavation and construction if they are to succeed.

A prairie garden pond can be installed during any frost-free period, but it is usually best to wait until autumn, when the days are warm with little rainfall. If you decide to excavate during months of heaviest

A lovely bridge provides an ideal spot to view the vibrant lilies (Nymphaea 'Attraction') and rockery plantings of this water garden.

A large country setting and good clay subsoil make possible this lovely earth pond. Plantings have been planned to mimic nature.

rainfall, keep a watchful eye on the weather and be prepared to cover the work area with a tarp or sturdy plastic. Several days of heavy rain can turn your partially dug pond into a morass.

Earth Ponds

In rural locations with good clay subsoil, a large earth pond may be the best choice because the amount of flexible pond liner required will be financially prohibitive, and the liner will, in any event, be prone to damage from recreational activities such as swimming in summer and skating in winter.

Earth ponds are subject to relatively high levels of seepage, so unless the water levels can be maintained from a natural spring, the location will have to take every advantage of natural drainage patterns. To position your pond you will have to search out a likely low-

lying area and then conscientiously observe runoff patterns to establish points of pond inflow and outflow. Ensure also that the location is readily accessible to the power equipment inevitably required for excavating a large pond.

A large well-stocked earth pond must be deep enough to overwinter hardy plant material and fish. Generally, the deepest point of the pond should be at least 6' (1.8 m).

CONSTRUCTING EARTH PONDS

1 Have local authorities mark the location of all underground utilities. Your survey of the site also should reasonably assure you that no old foundations or other large debris will hamper your pond construction.

2 Use a rope, garden hose or marking paint to outline the desired pond shape.

3 View the pond shape from all rel-

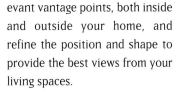

evant vantage points, both inside and outside your home, and refine the position and shape to provide the best views from your living spaces.

4 Excavate the deepest part of the pond to 6' (1.8 m) and gradually slope the edges toward the perimeter, leaving a shelf 18" (46 cm) wide and 8–12" (20–30 cm) deep for emergent plant material. Don't slope the pond so steeply that you'll have difficulty moving plant material about the pond. Continue to slope the perimeter, leaving a runoff channel at the lowest ground-level point, where a bog garden can be planted. Overflow from the pond must not interfere with your enjoyment of other areas of the garden.

5 Dampen and thoroughly pack the clay subsoil to improve water retention. A rented mechanical plate compactor will be of great assistance.

6 Add 1–3" (2.5–8 cm) of organic soil to provide a growing medium for aquatic plants.

7 Fill the pond from a natural water source if possible. If tap water must be used, allow several days for the chlorine to dissipate before adding plants.

8 Finish the edges of the pond with natural material, either grass or stones.

9 Follow the steps for balancing your pond (page 101) by adding an appropriate number of oxygenating and other plants at appropriate depths to establish an ecological balance.

10 After approximately one month, fish may be added.

Preformed Ponds

Preformed or molded ponds are excellent choices for smaller urban landscapes because they are durable and may be repaired if punctured. The pit for a preformed pond can typically be dug in a few hours without resorting to power equipment. Be warned, however, that the size of these ponds can be deceptive, looking quite large when resting in store displays, but seeming to shrink once installed in the garden. If a single pond is too small for your landscape, consider purchasing another and installing two ponds end to end several feet apart. Join them with an overhanging stone or wooden bridge to create the illusion of a continuous pond. Alternately, a preformed waterfall and stream channel can be used to join two or more ponds at different ground levels.

Manufactured from polyethylene or fiberglass, preformed ponds are available in a variety of styles and sizes—from informal free-form and kidney shapes complete with shelves for marginal plants, to rectangular, octagonal, circular or L-shapes for formal applications.

In the prairie climate, polyethylene tends to stand up better than fiberglass, but both are relatively durable and, most importantly, are resistant to the damaging effects of ultraviolet light. The life expectancy of superior preformed polyethylene pools is twenty years, while a quality fiberglass unit will last up to fifteen. Fiberglass, however, is more brittle and prone to pressure damage from ice.

INSTALLING PREFORMED PONDS

1 Have local authorities mark the location of all underground utilities. Your survey of the site also should reasonably assure you that no old foundations or other large debris will hamper your pond construction.

2 Lay the shell upside down over the proposed site and use powdered chalk to outline the shape.

3 View the pond shape from all relevant vantage points, both inside and outside your home, and refine the position to provide the best views from your living spaces.

4 Dig the pit about 3" (8 cm) larger than the outline to allow space for properly backfilling the pond later.

5 Dig the hole to conform with the shape of your pond. This can be somewhat tricky because preformed shells do not have uniform depth. Some trial and error fitting may be required.

6 Both the top and bottom of the pit must be level, so use a carpenter's level on a long board or a string level to check your progress.

7 Excavate to a depth 2" (5 cm) deeper than the preformed shell. Compact the clay at the base, and take care to remove any sharp objects that could damage the shell. Add 2" (5 cm) of sand to the bottom to cushion the shell. Wetting the sand will help hold it in place while forming it.

8 Lay the shell in the hole, sliding it back and forth to ensure the bottom makes contact at all points. The top rim of the shell must rest slightly above ground level to prevent surface runoff from entering the pond. Check the level again and add more sand if necessary.

9 Partially fill the pond with water to firmly situate it in place.

10 Backfill the shell with sand to the desired water level.

11 Add water and backfill in stages to protect the sides of the pond from bowing out under water pressure.

12 Stop filling about 2" (5 cm) from the top of the pond rim, and finish the edge with stone, brick or grass. If the pond is set into a deck, a wooden form will have to be constructed to prevent the sides from bowing out once it is completely filled with water.

13 Fill the pond to the top. If tap water must be used, let the pond sit for several days to allow the

chlorine to dissipate before adding aquatic plants.

14 Follow the steps for ecologically balancing your pond (page 101) by adding an appropriate number of oxygenating and other plants at appropriate depths.

15 After approximately one month, fish may be added.

Flexible Liner Ponds

Flexible liner ponds have become the most popular material for pond construction. Liners of butyl (isobutylene with isoprene), PVC (polyvinyl chloride) and EPDM (ethylene propylene diene monomer) compounds are available in virtually any size, and many retailers offer small and medium sizes precut, on the shelf, ready to take home.

The flexible pond liner offers several advantages to water gardeners. Because the material will conform to virtually any shape, it allows the greatest flexibility in pond design. Liners are probably the easiest of pond materials to install, and the top edge can be finished with a wide range of materials to suit virtually any design. Any minor variations in the level of the pond edge can be corrected after installation by simply packing sand under a low spot or by removing it from a high spot. Most pond liner material is relatively easy and inexpensive to repair in the event of a puncture. Liner materials vary in performance and price, but they are still the most economical method of pond construction.

A quality flexible pond liner, which should last twenty or more years, is the most economical choice over the long term. Poor quality liners may start to deteriorate after only a few years. Even worse is an old waterbed liner or any other synthetic material that will not resist the harmful effects of ultraviolet radiation.

Flexible pond liners do, however, require extra vigilance during installation. The liner's principal advantage of conforming to the shape of the excavation will become a disadvantage if the walls slump because of soft soil conditions. The liner also can be punctured by the roots of invasive plants and neighboring trees and by sharp implements or stones.

CHOOSING POND LINERS

Originally, polyethylene was the only flexible pond liner material available. It is still used occasionally because it is quite inexpensive, but it punctures easily and deteriorates rapidly in sunlight. Once polyethylene becomes brittle, it is virtually impossible to repair. The only satisfactory application of polyethylene is perhaps in large wildlife ponds, where economy is essential and the liner can be buried under a generous layer of soil to protect it from physical damage and ultraviolet degradation.

*A concrete-
bordered
perennial bed is
transformed into
a water feature.
Here, the feature
is being dug to
several depths to
accommodate
deep-water and
emergent plants.*

*A layer of sand
is added to cush-
ion the liner.*

*The liner is in the
process of being
installed.*

Natural stone and a rustic bridge finish the pond, which is now ready for planting. A Japanese-style waterspout in the upper left corner will add a gentle melody near the deck.

PVC is much stronger than polyethylene and has some resistance to ultraviolet light. With an estimated lifespan of ten to twelve years, PVC will outlast polyethylene, but it does become brittle with age and is difficult to repair once it has lost its elasticity. PVC is available in many sizes, and sheets can be heat welded together if required. For most backyard ponds, a thickness of 20 mil will be adequate.

PVC is only moderately puncture resistant and therefore should be installed over a generous layer of sand, felt, old carpet or similar underlays to protect it. PVC liners can be repaired by heat welding or by using PVC adhesive, which, since it bonds by chemical reaction, can

The illusion of space is created by constructing this freeform pond under the corner of a deck.

be used to make underwater repairs as long as the liner is still flexible.

Butyl or EPDM rubber is the most expensive option among flexible pond liners, but it is best suited to the often harsh prairie climate. Made with synthetic compounds, the material remains flexible to temperatures of −94°F (−70°C) even years after installation. Punctures can be repaired by heat welding or with butyl mastic tape. Butyl and EPDM liners are normally available only in black, but this is rarely a problem because a natural look is generally desirable in free-form ponds.

INSTALLING FLEXIBLE POND LINERS

1 Have local authorities mark the location of all underground utilities. Your survey of the site also should reasonably assure you that no old foundations or other large debris will hamper your pond construction.

2 Outline the desired shape of the pond. Mark informal ponds with powdered chalk, a rope or a garden hose. Choose gentle, sweeping lines and flowing curves that appear as if fashioned by nature. Simple shapes work best. For a circular pond use a central stake and string to circumscribe the line accurately. For a formal, four-sided pond, use stakes and string. To ensure square angles, use the carpenter's triangle rule: From the stake at the first corner, mark 3 units of measure (feet or meters) in one direction and 4 units in the other. When the diagonal measure between these points is 5 units, the angle is exactly 90°. Whatever the pond's shape, be sure to view it from all angles inside and outside your home, and adjust the shape or position as required. Mark planting shelves for marginal aquatic plants as a

gentle reminder not to dig the entire pond to one level. Shelves for these marginal plants should be about 9–12" (23–30 cm) wide and 8–12" (20–30 cm) deep.

3 Dig down to the first shelf. The sides of the pond should slope inward at about a 30° angle. The ratio is 3" (7.5 cm) of incline for each 10" (25 cm) of depth. If the soil is loose, make the marginal shelves wider and use a more gradual slope.

4 Use a spirit level on a straight piece of lumber laid across the excavation or a string level anchored to a stake to ensure that both the rim of the pond and the marginal shelf are level. If the level must be adjusted, it is best to excavate the higher segment rather than building up the lower because it's difficult to pack freshly dug earth sufficiently.

5 Continue excavating until you have reached the desired depth. Pond depth can be checked during digging by laying a straight board across the hole and measuring down to be bottom with a tape measure. For thriving water lilies 18–26" (46–66 cm) of depth is sufficient. If you plan to overwinter lilies in the pond, the depth will have to be increased to 3.25–6.5' (1–2 m), depending on your climatic zone. Excavate about 2" (5 cm) deeper and wider than the final pond size to allow for the addition of sand to cush-

ion the liner. Bear in mind that a pond deeper than 2' (61 cm) may be subject to swimming pool safety bylaws. Check local ordinances to determine if you will be required to fence the pond area.

6 The rim of the pond should be 8–12" (20–30 cm) wide. It should also be several inches above ground level and slope gently away from the pond to prevent runoff from fouling the water. A shallow ledge 12–15" (30–38 cm) wide can be cut beyond the rim for final finishing with edging material that will hide the excess liner. A slit trench also can be dug around the rim to accept bog plants.

7 The base of your new pond should be relatively smooth with approximately a 10° slope to the deepest end. A spirit level on a straight piece of lumber or a string level can be used to check the slope. For every 10" (25 cm) of length the pond should drop 1" (2.5 cm) toward the deepest end.

8 The sides and bottom of the excavation should be closely inspected for any sharp objects such as rocks or tree roots that may damage the liner when filled.

9 The entire excavation can now be lined with about 2" (5 cm) of damp sand to cushion and protect the liner. An additional underlay of geotextile, a spun poly-

Pond construction. Excavate pond to desired shape and form shelves for emergent plants.

Drape flexible liner over hole, use rocks to hold liner in place and start to fill pond with water.

Position desired edging around pond and trim excess liner.

The pond is ready for aquatic plant material.

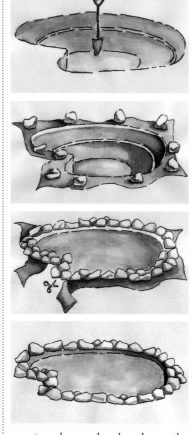

ester, also can be placed over the sand before the liner is installed. Good quality underlay is not cheap, but it will help protect the liner from many punctures. Old, synthetic carpeting with a thickness of 1/2" (1 cm) is an acceptable alternative to a commercial underlay. If your design includes the placement of heavy rocks in the pond, you should install a concrete block or pad beneath the flexible liner to provide extra support.

10 To calculate the final liner size, add twice the depth to the measurements for the length and width, and then add 2' (61 cm) for the edge. For example, a pond 4' (1.2 m) wide by 6' (1.8 m) long and 2' (61 cm) deep will require a liner 10' x 12' (3 x 3.7 m).

11 Place the liner in the center of the hole, unfold it, and begin to smooth it out. Work the liner until it evenly overlaps all sides of the pond by about 12" (30 cm). At this point you can make the initial folds and tucks for curves and corners. To make the liner more pliable and easier to position, lay it in the warm sun for a few hours.

12 Place rocks or bricks around the rim to anchor the liner and begin to fill the pond with water. Adjust the rocks or bricks as the pond fills and the liner begins to stretch and settle. (If you are on a water meter, this is the perfect opportunity to determine the water volume of your pond. Check the meter reading prior to filling and again when the pond is full. This information can be useful if you plan to add commercial fertilizers later.)

13 Stop filling the pond when the water level reaches 2–4" (5–10 cm) below ground level. Work out any remaining wrinkles and pleat corners and curves.

14 Fold the liner over the rim of the pond, leaving 12" (30 cm) of material to anchor the top of the liner. Bury or trim any excess as required.

15 Finish the periphery of the pond with edging that will conceal the liner and hold it in place.

16 Fill the pond to the top. If tap water has been used, wait several days for chlorine to dissipate before adding plants.

Concrete Ponds

The use of concrete for pond construction has rapidly declined with advent of durable synthetic materials, but it remains one of the most adaptable mediums. Nevertheless, the complexities of working with concrete may necessitate the services of a professional contractor, substantially increasing the cost of construction. It is also is difficult to finish concrete to achieve the natural effect preferred for an informal style, and because it does not flex like other liners, it is prone to frost damage in the harsh prairie climate. Once the pond has cracked, permanent repair is very difficult. Often the only workable solution is to install a flexible pond liner inside the concrete shell. This alone is enough to dissuade most prairie gardeners from installing a concrete pond.

Another drawback to concrete is the lime it contains. Before you can add aquatic plant or animal life, it must be cured to prevent harmful lime from leaching into the water. This can be accomplished with pH buffering compounds, a commercial lime neutralizer, a lengthy process of water changes or with pool paint.

To make a newly constructed concrete pond safe for aquatic plants and animals, fill the pond with fresh water, wait twenty-four hours and then drain. Repeat the procedure at least three or four times, letting the water stand one week before draining a final time. After the final filling, aquatic plants can be safely added, but only if nonchlorinated water has been used. Otherwise, you will have to wait several days to allow the chlorine to dissipate.

If you are still intent on a concrete pond, consult an experienced professional for advice on adequately reinforcing the structure during construction and protecting it from frost damage during the winter.

Edging Ponds

The pond's perimeter must be edged to hide the liner. To create a sense of unity, the edging materials should complement the style of your pond and should be similar to those used elsewhere in your garden. For example, a pond situated close to a Rundle stone patio should use the same material for the edging. A pond with an informal style is best edged with natural stone. A more formal design favors edging of finished materials such as sandstone, limestone or marble, or manufactured material such as brick, tile, concrete or treated lumber. If your budget is tight, concrete patio slabs also can be used.

Position edging material over the

*FORMAL BRICK EDGE.
This combination
of bricks
effectively hides
the pond liner.*

*REINFORCED STONE
EDGE. Emergent
plants between
stones hide the
pond liner.*

*BOG GARDEN EDGE.
The pond keeps
the bog moist
and the stone
dam prevents soil
from washing
into pond.*
*BOG GARDEN EDGE.
The liner, punc-
tured to allow
drainage, extends
under bog.
Boulders keep
soil in place.*
*GRASS OR TURF EDGE.
The natural
landscape blends
with the pond's
surface. Soil
hides liner.*

*WOOD EDGE. Treated
lumber hides
liner nicely and
is less formal
than concrete,
brick or cut stone.*

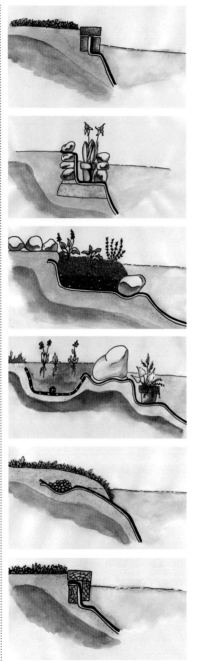

second layer of edging material over the first. This will completely hide the liner and protect it from punctures. Whichever edge treatment you choose you must ensure the rim of the pond is above ground level to prevent leakage or seepage.

If your site is very sandy or if heavy foot traffic is expected around the pond, the edge should be strengthened with a 6" (15 cm) layer of gravel, bricks or concrete beneath the edging. The edging should overhang the pond by about 2" (5 cm) to help conceal the liner and protect it from ultraviolet light.

If you wish to attract birds to your pond, consider finishing one edge with a sand or pebble beach. The antics of robins will be a source of entertainment as they rush into the pond, splash in the water, and then run back up the beach to vigorously shake before taking the plunge again. Beware, however, that a pebble beach will be irresistible to small children, who will delight in tossing your entire pebble beach into the pond one pebble at a time.

A bog garden is a functional and decorative way to disguise the edge of the liner. It introduces a new spectrum of plants to the water garden and will attract amphibians. To create a bog garden dig a gently sloping trench at least 2–3' (61–91 cm) wide immediately adjacent to the pond. Add a punctured liner to supply drainage and fill with heavy, dampened bog soil.

liner at the pond's edge, and then wrap the excess liner over the edging material. Position a layer of underlay on top of the liner before placing the

Recipe for Bog Soil

Bog soil must contain enough organic material to readily retain the moisture required by water-loving plants. An ideal mixture contains equal parts of peat or sphagnum moss and good garden loam. At any time, you should be able to squeeze a handful of it and release some moisture.

Stocking Ponds with Fish

As a general rule the smaller the pond the more it will be susceptible to large fluctuations in temperature, so it is wise to monitor the pond for several weeks to ensure that the temperature falls within the acceptable range for fish. Hardy goldfish are typically comfortable in a wide range of temperatures, from just above freezing to as high as 85°F (29°C). The beautiful but less resilient koi require temperatures between 50–85°F (10–29°C). At less than 60°F (16°C) koi become sluggish.

If your pond warms to above the acceptable level for fish, add more deep-water and floating plants to shade the surface. Generally, shading 50 percent of the pond's surface should keep the temperature at an acceptable level. If this does not prove sufficient, add more tall plants such as cattails and rushes on the south side of the pond to increase the amount of shade. If fish are distressed and gasping for air, you may have to take the emergency measure of adding cool water to the pond, or running your fountain or waterfall continuously to cool the water and provide additional oxygen for the fish.

Waterfalls, Streams and Fountains

Incorporating moving water into your water feature brings added

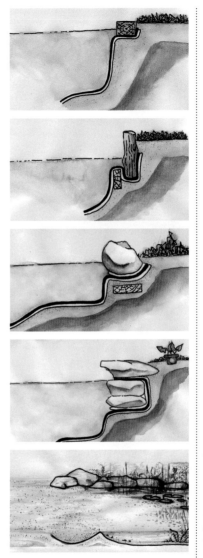

Variation for a wood edge. Thick, treated timber hides liner.

Variation for a wood edge. Upright posts are sandwiched between treated lumber and soil.

Rock edges. Rocks create an informal effect while containing the pond and hiding the liner. Two methods are shown. Necessary to each is a firm base of treated timber or rocks to sustain the weight of the rock edging.

Sand beach edge. Small mammals and birds that enjoy bathing and playing in shallow water will be attracted.

The strong lines and angles of this formal waterfall complement the rectangular pool below and the terrace and benches above.

aesthetic and practical benefits. Water cascading from a fountain or over a falls or gently babbling in a stream is a delight to both the eye and ear. Apart from their aesthetic beauty, waterfalls, streams and fountains help aerate and purify the water in your pond.

Any moving water element in your garden will tend to dominate, so it's essential that its design complement the style of your pond. For example, because nature creates no fountains except geysers, fountains should be restricted to formally styled pools. Waterfalls spilling into formal ponds should appear architectural with curved lines and straight angles. Conversely, a waterfall in an informal pond should reflect the irregular shapes of nature.

Waterfalls, streams and fountains must be carefully planned and constructed to prevent spillage or leakage, to reduce the impact of evaporation and to create ideal growing conditions for water plants. Any moving water feature is subject to high rates of evaporation, so it must be in proportion with your pond or you may face the prospect of constantly topping up the water level.

Water plants, especially the coveted water lilies, thrive best in still water, so the volume of your waterfall and your planting strategy will have to be adjusted accordingly. To reduce the velocity of a waterfall as it flows into the main pond, consider constructing a large separate basin just a few inches above water level. Similarly, the volume of water produced by fountains or streams may have to be restricted, and they may have to be positioned well away from still-water plants.

Waterfall and stream units can be purchased preformed or can be constructed from natural materials laid over a flexible liner. Preformed waterfall and stream units are constructed of the same synthetics as preformed ponds and are durable in the prairie climate. An added advantage is that the engineering has been done for you. With proper installation and the correct volume of water, they will perform nicely. Their drawbacks include expense, a limited range of styles and sizes (whether as one-piece or stackable units) and an artificial appearance that is often difficult to camouflage with plantings or natural materials.

Waterfalls or streams constructed of flexible liners made of butyl or EPDM are very durable and afford the greatest opportunity for informal designs that approximate the work of nature. They require, however, thoughtful planning and careful construction to avoid spillage or leakage. Ideally, your waterfall will be designed as a series of small pools linked by cascading water.

Designing a stream presents special problems. If, for example, it simply starts at the top of a berm, it will look unnatural, so it is preferable for a stream to connect two or more ponds through a graceful series of meanders. The size of the ponds and the capacity of the stream and pump must be carefully balanced to prevent flooding the lower pond while leaving an inadequate supply of water in the upper pond when the pump is turned off.

Fountains and catchment basins are readily available in a wide range of styles and materials. They are easy to install, but they can be expensive and must be carefully matched to the output of your pump to achieve the desired effect. Seek professional advice to determine the pump capacity that best suits your fountain.

INSTALLING PREFORMED WATERFALLS

1 Using soil from the pond excavation, create a mound into which the waterfall unit will be set. Tamp and level the soil.

2 Position the one-piece unit or the base of the overlapping units on the foundation, ensuring that it sufficiently overhangs the pond. Place additional units appropriately as desired, again ensuring adequate overhang. It is always wise to insert a piece of flexible liner between the units to channel any water that goes astray. The liner can eventually be hidden by plants or natural materials placed around the waterfall.

3 Position the pump hose to run up the back or side of the preformed waterfall where it can be hidden by the soil. Be especially careful not to crimp or crush the hose.

4 Carefully level the unit, and then run water through it to test its performance. Make adjustments as required.

5 Secure the preformed waterfall in place by firmly tamping earth

around it. Wooden stakes will provide additional support.

6 The waterfall edges and any exposed liner can now be covered with rocks and soil. Plants can be positioned around the falls to blend the structure into the surrounding landscape. Creeping rockery plants such as Kamtschaticum stonecrop *(Sedum Kamtschaticum)*, thyme *(Thymus serpyllum)*, bearberry or Kinnikinick *(Arctostaphylos uva-ursi)*, mock strawberry *(Duchesnea indica)* and creeping baby's breath *(Gypsophila repens)* will camouflage the waterfall edges and provide a range of foliage and color. Small plants may also be quite interesting in this setting. Try alpine columbine *(Aquilegia alpina)*, pinks *(Dianthus deltoides)*, and hens and chicks *(Sempervivum* spp.).

Installing Preformed Streams

1 Working from the reservoir pool, place the preformed unit upside down in the desired location and mark the edges with powdered chalk.

2 Dig a gently sloping shallow trench 2" (5 cm) wider and deeper than the preformed unit. Keeping the slope gradual will ensure that some water will remain in the stream in the event of a pump failure.

3 Prepare a damp, tamped sand base, and set the unit in place

with the discharge lip overlapping the edge of the pond.

4 Repeat the process for each preformed unit up to the top (header) pool. The discharge lip of each unit must overlap the one below it.

5 Dig a trench about 6" (15 cm) deep alongside the stream to hide the water delivery pipe.

6 Test the stream before backfilling the stream units and water delivery pipe. Ensure that the water flows smoothly from unit to unit without any spillage. Make adjustments as needed.

7 Backfill the stream units with sand, and add a layer of topsoil for rockery or alpine plants to camouflage the units.

Installing Flexible Liner Waterfalls

1 Using soil from the pond excavation, create a mound of well-tamped soil.

2 Starting at the lowest level, construct a series of shallow catchment pools through which water will flow naturally. The sides of the pools must be built up sufficiently to contain splashing.

3 Install liners into each catchment basin, ensuring that each significantly overlaps the one below it to prevent capillary action from drawing water out of the system.

4 Line the edges of each catchment basin with flat stones, tilting the ones at the front slightly forward to ensure that the water falls

freely from basin to basin. The front stones or spout also must overhang the basin below.

5 Test the waterfall and make adjustments as required.

6 To tune the melody of your waterfall, adjust the distance between the catchment pools, change the amount that stones overhang each basin and alter the volume of water. Experiment until your waterfall has a pleasant, musical echo.

7 Carefully tamp soil around the falls and create spaces for plantings that will camouflage the exterior of the system.

8 Hide the waterfall edges and any exposed liner with rocks and soil.

9 Add plants around the waterfall to blend it into the surrounding landscape. Large waterfalls can benefit from coniferous shrubs available in a variety of shapes and sizes. For smaller waterfalls try dwarf junipers, creeping ground covers and ornamental grasses. Since many informal water gardens are designed to take on the character of alpine scenes, many dwarf alpine and rockery plants are also ideal for planting around waterfalls.

TUNING WATERFALLS

A waterfall should create a pleasing melody that is neither too loud nor too soft. If after installing your waterfall, the sound is not pleasing, there are several ways to tune it.

The most obvious adjustment is to increase or decrease the flow of water from the pump to the drop point. Some pumps have a dial on the housing to adjust the water volume. With others you may have to use hose clamps on the output hose to adjust the volume. You should, however, never restrict the intake of the pump because this

This waterfall's flat stone spillway can be adjusted forward and backward to tune the sound of cascading water. One of the biggest challenges is to get water to flow over rather than under the spout. Try packing sand under the liner to make it better conform to the spout's shape. Nontoxic spray foam also can be used under the spout to prevent leakage.

A large stream under construction with liner in place.

can damage the pump and void the warranty.

The second method of altering the sound is to use rock with a different surface texture. Water flowing over or onto smooth rocks makes less noise because it clings to the surface as it moves. Rocks with a coarse surface produce the opposite effect.

A third potential adjustment is to change the water's angle of descent. Water cascading freely at a 90° angle to the water's surface will be louder and sound less natural than water flowing over rocks at a more gradual angle.

Echo chambers behind the falls provide a fourth opportunity to tune the sound. These spaces, like an acoustic guitar body, amplify and bring resonance to the sound through echoes. To adjust the chambers behind a waterfall, simply increase or decrease the amount of rock overhanging each basin.

The final method of tuning a waterfall is particularly suited to more formal water features and is applied frequently indoors. This technique uses a guide for the water to travel over. For example, in a small wall fountain a clear fishing line could be strung between the mouth of the fountain and a rock beneath the water's surface. The water will glide gently along the line and enter the pond with barely a sound. Outdoor features can produce the same effect by directing water down a smooth surface.

INSTALLING FLEXIBLE LINER STREAMS

1 Using rope or garden hose, mark the edges of a meandering stream to flow between the upper header and lower reservoir pools.

2 Starting at the lower reservoir pool, dig a trench 2" (5 cm) wider and deeper than required.

3 Add a 2" (5 cm) layer of dampened sand to the trench.

4 Since a single piece of liner will be difficult to fit around tight curves, cut the liner into several sections and install them with overlaps just as you would shingle a roof. If you desire, the overlapping liner sections can be sealed with butyl tape.

5 Conceal the edges of the liner with the same natural or manufactured materials used around your ponds.

Pumps, Fountains, Heaters and Filters

Modern compact submersible pumps are readily affordable, easy to install and maintain, and available in a large range of output capacities. Performance is measured in the number of U.S. gallons pumped per hour and the maximum number of feet water can be lifted. Maximum lift, also known as "head," is the greatest height that the pump can lift water. The higher the pump has to lift the water, the less its output.

Before selecting a pump, measure the amount of lift and estimate the volume of flow your water feature will require, and then seek expert advice at a garden center. A pump with a capacity of 150–300 U.S. gallons (570–1135 l) per hour is typically enough to sustain a small waterfall or fountain several feet high.

Purchase a pump with greater output than you believe you will need so that you can adjust the out-

This formal fountain is the dominant feature of a simple turf-bordered pool.

Pond Construction Materials

Type	Cost	Durability	Ease of Installation	Design Flexibility	Repair	Other
Polyethylene Liner	Low	Poor	Easy	Good	Difficult	Short lifespan
PVC Liner	Low – medium	Fair – good	Easy	Good	Possible if not brittle	Easily punctured; finding holes is difficult
Butyl/EPDM Liner	Medium – high	Very good	Easy	Excellent	Possible at all times	Long lifespan
Preformed Pond	High	Fair – good	Difficult	Very limited	Possible with most materials	Expensive relative to size
Concrete	Very high	Depends on climate and workmanship	Requires professional installation	Very good	Difficult to keep watertight	Lime creates additional work

put and use diverters to split the output in two. Alternately, you can restrict the output with a clamp placed on the outlet side of the pump. Never restrict the pump at its intake point because this will cause wear and premature failure. Also, be aware that pump performance is reduced by the number of fittings and the length of hoses in the system, and by clogged filters and aging.

Place the submersible pump as close to your fountain as possible. This will ensure the greatest amount of lift while keeping strong water currents from other parts of the pond. Remember that moving water and still-water plants do not mix. If your heart is set on water lilies surrounding a fountain, you may have to limit the volume of the fountain or increase the size of the pond. Always position the pump away from objects that could restrict the intake.

Convenient access to an electrical outlet is necessary. The outlet must be a ground fault circuit interrupter (GFCI). The line leading to the receptacle should be 2–12 NMWU outdoor wire buried a minimum of 2' (61 cm).

Formally styled ponds will benefit from the addition of a fountain. The many styles available produce a variety of shapes such as a waterfalls, water lilies, single daisies, double daisies and foaming jets. Some kits include a number of jets, so you can change the effect whenever you want. When selecting a jet, bear in mind that extremely fine jets of water are lost in large landscapes and that small nozzles are prone to plugging with debris. Geyser jets, which provide large, continuously changing columns of foaming water, are not as prone to clogging but may be disrupted by wind. Fountain nozzles can be threaded onto submersible pumps quickly and easily, but it is wise to select a single manufacturer for both components to ensure that outlet size and thread patterns match.

Ornamental fountains also are available in an extensive variety of styles to complement any water garden design. Frogs, rabbits, lion heads and cherubs are common examples, but gargoyles, multi-level bowls and even classic or contemporary sculptures can be considered.

To overwinter plant material or fish in small water gardens, you may want to install a floating stock tank heater. At a few degrees above freezing, its thermostat activates a heating element, which provides a small ice-free area. This allows oxygen to enter the pond and toxic gases to escape. Installation is easy, but you must secure the heating element away from the pond liner. A continuously operating 1,500-watt heater can be expensive, so to conserve energy you may want to turn it on manually when temperatures threaten to freeze over the pond.

Filtration systems may be added

to help nature maintain an ecological balance in your pond. Mechanical filters, which simply trap unwanted debris as it is pumped through a filtering agent, can be effective, but biological filters are of more interest to today's water gardeners.

Active biological filters pump water through a filtering tank much like mechanical filters, but the key to their efficiency is bacteria. Microscopic armies of it break down ammonia and harmful pathogens, converting them to beneficial nitrates that fish and plants can use.

Passive biological filters introduce the same helpful bacteria directly into the pond. One trend advocates placing a large number of rocks on the floor of the pond. Their surfaces become hosts for the bacteria that clean the water by consuming the excessive nutrients that promote algae blooms. Some water garden centers now sell dehydrated bacteria to establish these colonies of biological cleaners.

Although filtration systems can be effective, they require frequent cleaning, and they keep you from addressing the reason for the problem—too few oxygenating plants, too many fish, not enough sunlight and so on. Some patience and experimentation with different variables should resolve most problems.

Pond Lighting

Low-voltage lighting around your pond extends the hours of viewing pleasure and creates a romantic ambiance in the garden at night, accenting plant foliage, ornaments, statuary and garden structures.

For safety, durability and ease of maintenance choose only quality systems designed for outdoor use. For most small to medium-sized ponds, a low-voltage system will provide adequate light. These use a transformer to step 110-volt current down to 12-volt. The system should plug into a ground fault circuit interrupter (GFCI) receptacle.

When planning lighting, look to nature for inspiration. Mimic moonlight with low-voltage fixtures shining down from trees on favorite plants or statuary. Aim the lights at the back or sides of the pond rather than directly at the water's surface. The indirect lighting will turn the surface into a dark reflecting mirror. Uplight objects such as fountains or waterfalls to provide focal points. Fish, however, may be bothered by light, so ensure that a portion of the pond remains dark when nightlighting is used.

CHAPTER 3

Planting Water Gardens

W ATER-LOVING PLANTS ADD both practicality and beauty to the water garden. With the proper number and variety of plants, your pond will establish an ecological balance that will keep algae blooms to a minimum.

Water and bog garden plants are available in a wide variety of forms, colors and textures to suit any garden style. A formal geometric water garden finished with manufactured materials such as brick or tile may feature a number of splendid exotic water lilies. The sweeping lines of an informal garden, on the other hand, may favor a wild tangle of natural species in the pond and on its margins.

Your pond and its margins will be home for a number of plants. Every plant will belong to one of five major groups: marginal, emergent,

The pale green foliage of common duckweed (Lemna minor) dramatically contrasts the foliage and color of this Nymphaea 'Escarboucle' lily.

Study nature in the wild before planting your water garden. Here, a woodland setting gives way to shrubs, grasses, emergent plants and deep-water species.

submerged, deep-water and free-floating. Each group has a distinct habitat.

It's wise before beginning to plant your water garden to take a field trip to a pond in the wild and study how natural ponds include plants from the five groups. Marginal aquatic varieties (often referred to as bog plants) grow in the soggy soil on the banks of ponds, streams and islands. Emergent aquatic plants grow in the shallow water near the pond's edge. Only their leaves rise above the water's surface; their roots remain firmly planted in the soil below. Submerged plants (also called oxygenators) grow completely underwater,

but send leaves near the water's surface for sunlight. Deep-water plants grow in the soil in deep areas of the pond, but their leaves, supported by stems of up to several feet in length, grow on and above the water. Lilies are among the most common deep-water plants. Because their leaves float on the water's surface, deep-water plants are often classed with the fifth group of aquatic plants, the free-floating varieties, which do not need soil, but simply float on the water's surface.

Your pond will need to imitate these growing environments with shelves for emergent and submerged plants, adequate depth for

deep-water species and perhaps overflow channels to keep bog gardens moist. Free-floating plants, of course, will require adequate surface area to thrive.

A number of aquatic varieties are available in each group, and many have been hybridized to provide gardeners with an extensive selection of colorful blooms and interesting foliage. More and more aquatic plant retailers sell native aquatic plants in addition to hybrids.

The water garden should be planted in the spring or no later than early summer if plants are to blossom and be enjoyed that season. Plants in the bog garden, such as irises, can be planted in the autumn.

Marginal Plants

The plant material in this zone has adapted to the boggy saturated soil at the edge of the pond or to a limited depth of water cover. Generally, these plants can handle short-term fluctuations in water level. Grasses and rushes are the most common plants found in this zone, and there are many varieties to choose from. Several species recommended for prairie water gardens include marsh reed grass (*Calamagrostis canadensis*) and cattails (*Typha* spp.). Marsh reed grass has numerous thin spikelike leaves and 4' (1.2 m) -tall stems topped by nodding tussocks, which look very natural hanging over the

Left: Spike rush (Eleocharis palustris)

Right: Pink flowering rush (Butomus umbellatus)

Left: Yellow marsh marigold (Caltha palustris)

Right: Dwarf cattail (Typha minima)

pond's edge. Planted *en masse* the marsh reed can provide a gentle backdrop for accent specimens with a coarser texture such as the cattail. These erect perennials with cylindrical brown flowerheads and graceful straplike leaves grow to about 2–2.5' (61–76 cm) tall. Both these plants can be invasive and should be restricted to the bog garden or to pots to keep them from roaming too freely.

To provide a burst of early spring color in the bog garden, consider the marsh marigold *(Caltha palustris)* or its smaller cousin the alpine marsh marigold *(Caltha leptosepala)*. The marsh marigold, one of our personal favorites, grows 10–14" (25–36 cm) tall and has vibrant deep yellow blooms. Shortly after the crocuses and daffodils in the rest of your garden have faded, your bog garden will be awash with the brilliant blooms of these gorgeous native plants. The alpine marsh marigold features white flowers tinged with blue or mauve atop 6–12" (15–30 cm) stalks. As the flowers die back, the waxy green heart-shaped leaves of both species form a coarse-looking mound, which will contrast nicely with plants of finer textures. Frogs and other wildlife love to seek refuge in the shade of marginal plants.

Other native varieties ideally suited to the margin of the pond include sedges *(Carex* spp.), spike rush *(Eleocharis palustris)*, Siberian iris

Left: Kermesina water iris (Iris versicolor *var.* 'Kermesina')

Right: Japanese *iris* (Iris kaempferi)

(Iris sibirica), watercress *(Nasturtium officinale),* palmate-leaved coltsfoot *(Petasites palmatus),* arrow-leaved coltsfoot *(Petasites sagittatus),* western dock *(Rumex occidentalis)* and arum-leaved arrowhead *(Sagittaria cuneata).*

Over one hundred varieties of grasslike sedges grow throughout the prairies. One of the most distinctive is the golden sedge *(Carex aurea).* Its flowers, borne on spikes 6–12" (15–30 cm) tall, appear as a pale greenish yellow but turn a rich reddish brown as the fruit matures.

Spike rush has 4–40" (10–100 cm) -long leafless cylindrical stems tipped with brown spikelets.

Irises are highly favored marginal plants for their form, texture and color. One of the best choices for prairie water gardens is the Siberian iris, which features white, mauve or pale-blue blooms atop 2–4' (61–122 cm) -tall stems. It is best planted *en masse* or as a bold accent.

Watercress sports numerous tiny white flowers on stalks 12" (30 cm) in height. It sends out runners that root at every node, similar to the strawberry plant.

Both species of coltsfoot have prominent, distinctive foliage and bear rays of white flowers on stalks 6–18" (15–46 cm) tall. They are among the first water plants to bloom in the spring.

Resembling its cousin the garden rhubarb, western dock grows 2–5' (61–152 cm) high. Its tiny pale green

*Arrowhead
(Sagittaria
cuneata)*

flowers form long, dense clusters that turn a rich reddish brown later in the season.

The arum-leaved arrowhead derives its name from the shape of its prominent leaves, which grow 2–8" (5–20 cm) long. White, showy flowers bloom on stalks 8–16" (20–41 cm) tall.

Emergent Plants

Emergent plants, which enjoy wet feet and dry heads, are adapted to the shallow water near the edges of ponds or slow-moving streams. Emergent species prefer a constant water level, but can withstand the occasional flood as long as they are not totally submerged. As with bog plants, most emergent species are perennials and can survive prairie winters.

Although emergent plants generally require a minimum water depth of 2" (5 cm), ideal planting depths for each species vary significantly. Therefore, it's wise to grow them in containers that can be positioned at optimum depths on bricks or rocks that can be easily camouflaged.

Some excellent options for your prairie water garden include flowering rush (*Butomus umbellatus*), common scouring rush (*Equisetum hyemale*), yellow water iris (*Iris pseudacorus*), blue water iris (*Iris versicolor*), mare's tail (*Hippuris vulgaris*), pencil cattail (*Typha angustifolia*), common cattail (*Typha latifolia*), floating marsh marigold

Left: Yellow water iris (Iris pseudacorus)

Right: Blue water iris (Iris laevigata)

(*Caltha nathans*), water smartweed (*Polygonum amphibium*), broad-leaved pondweed (*Potamogeton natans*), white water crowfoot (*Ranunculus aquatilis*) and yellow water crowfoot (*Ranunculus gmelinii*).

The flowering rush has long, narrow leaves and rose-pink flowers 1" (2.5 cm) across that radiate like the stays of an umbrella on 3' (91 cm) stalks.

The common scouring rush has tall, erect stalks with jointed bamboolike stems 4' (1.2 m) high ending in pointed, cone-shaped spikes containing spores.

The yellow water iris is worth growing for its graceful swordlike blue-green foliage, which reaches heights of 3' (91 cm). Its yellow flowers are marked with darker veins and centers. Equally beautiful is the blue water iris, distinguished by an abundance of violet-blue flowers branching along 2' (61 cm) stems. As the blooms fade, the plant forms an attractive mound of narrow gray-green leaves.

Mare's tail has whorls of spikey leaves along narrow stalks that grow 18–20" (46–51 cm) above the water.

The common cattail is by far the best-known native marsh plant. Its long swordlike leaves sheath the base of a stock 4–6' (1.2–1.8 m) tall and ending in the characteristic deep brown spike. Its taller cousin, the pencil cattail grow 6–8' (1.8–2.4 m)

Top: White water crowfoot (Ranunculus aquatilis)

Bottom: Yellow water crowfoot (Ranunculus gmelinni)

and has much narrower leaves. The common cattail is best reserved for larger earthen ponds, but graceful pencil cattail makes a lovely addition to smaller ponds and even containers, where it provides a dramatic accent.

The floating marsh marigold is smaller than its bog garden cousins and is best suited to shallow water. Its tiny white flowers are interspersed among waxy green leaves growing along a vinelike stem.

Water smartweed is a hardy native that produces long, branching stems with lance-shaped leaves and attractive bright rose-colored flower spikelets.

Broad-leaved pondweed has nondescript flowers, but sports

showy reddish bronze oval-shaped leaves.

White and yellow water crowfoot are members of the buttercup family and are characterized by dense foliage and small, showy flowers on slender stalks. The leaves of the white water species are numerous and threadlike while those of the yellow water crowfoot are kidney-shaped and deeply lobed.

Submerged Aquatic Plants

Submerged aquatic plants perform an essential role in the pond by absorbing carbon dioxide and by releasing the oxygen necessary for thriving plant and animal life. Often referred to as oxygenators, they also compete with algae for nutrients and help keep the water clear. Some fine-textured species provide an ideal place for fish to spawn in safety, and bushy species help camouflage pots, pumps and hoses on the bottom of the pond.

Great oxygenators for your prairie water garden are Canadian pondweed (*Elodea canadensis*), hornwort (*Ceratophyllum demersum*) and common bladderwort (*Utricularia vulgaris* var. *americana*).

Canadian pondweed has dense whorls of spikelike leaves along the length of its narrow stalks.

The hornwort has threadlike leaves that fork off stems 16–59" (40–150 cm) long.

The bladderwort is one of the most fascinating shallow-water plants. It is a carnivore that supplements its nitrogen-poor diet by trapping insects and other small organisms. The bladders attached to the many leaves on its long, branching stems provide flotation but also open suddenly to snare insects. The leafless stalks grow above water and display several showy, bright yellow snapdragon-like flowers.

Water hyacinth (Eichhornia crassipes)

Broad-leaved
pondweed
(Potamogeton
natans)

Deep-Water Aquatic Plants

Deep-water aquatic plants such as water lilies are rooted, whereas free-floating aquatics such as duckweed are nonrooted. Common to both are leaves that lie on the water's surface, keeping the water shaded and discouraging algae growth.

Lilies are the undisputed stars of the water garden. They are available in a wide variety of colors and sizes, ranging from the small, unpretentious native yellow pond lily (Nuphar variegatum) to the dramatic tropical N. 'Comanche,' whose soft pink blooms transform into orange-red at the center until they look as if somehow illuminated from within.

Some excellent lilies for your water garden include N. 'Aurora,' N. 'Gonnère,' N. 'Madame Wilfron Gonnère,' N. 'Texas Dawn' and N. 'Virginia.' All water lilies have broad, floating leaves that vary in color from green to mottled green-brown.

The yellow-apricot blooms of the hardy N. 'Sioux' turn deep orange-red over a bloom period extending from June to October, weather permitting. With a spread of approximately 30" (76 cm), it is a perfect specimen plant for small ponds and container water gardens.

N. 'Gonnère' produces a magnificent full double white blossom with almost translucent outer petals. With plenty of sunshine it will bloom late into the afternoon. It is an excellent addition in medium to large ponds.

Water Lilies: Stars of the Water Garden

Yellow pond lily (Nuphar variegatum)

Comanche (Nymphaea 'Comanche')

Gloire du Temple-sur-Lot (Nymphaea 'Gloire du Temple-sur-Lot')

Common white
water lily
(Nymphaea 'Alba')

Yellow pygmy
(Nymphaea
pygmaea *var.*
'Helvola')

Fabiola
(Nymphaea
'Fabiola')
(*formerly*
Nymphaea 'Mrs.
Richmond')

Darwin
(Nymphaea
'Darwin')

Pink Gonnère
(Nymphaea
'Madame Wilfron
Gonnère')

William B. Shaw
(Nymphaea
'William B.
Shaw')

Rose Arey
(Nymphaea 'Rose
Arey')

Laydekeri fulgens
(Nymphaea
laydekeri
'Fulgens')

Perry's Baby Red
(Nymphaea
'Perry's Baby
Red')

*Escarboucle
(Nymphaea
'Escarboucle')*

*Naturalized pink
water lilies*

N. 'Madame Wilfron Gonnère' has a beautiful pink peonylike flowers. In the cooler weather of spring, the leaves exhibit a broad yellow stripe that fades as the warmer weather arrives.

N. 'Texas Dawn' is one the most perfect yellow water lilies. A prolific bloomer, its flowers are full with long, slender brilliant yellow petals. In the late summer the flower may take on a pinkish hue.

N. 'Virginia' produces white booms with long, slender petals. The innermost petals are pale yellow while the outer petals are white.

Unlike many other plants in the pond environment, most deepwater species are not native to the prairies, so it's a good idea to favor retailers who sell plants propagated in your area. You will likely have greater success than with newly imported plants.

Hardy water lilies can be overwintered in your pond as long as it does not freeze solid and they are moved to the bottom of the pond.

Free-Floating Plants

Free-floating plants roam freely across the pond with the currents and breezes. Like lilies, they prevent algae blooms by providing shade and competing for nutrients. A prairie water gardener can choose from a number of interesting imported and native species. Some excellent exotics to try include water hyacinth (*Eichhornia cras-*

sipes), frogbit (*Hydrocharis morsus-ranae*), water lettuce (*Pistia stratiotes*) and water soldier (*Stratiotes aloides*). It is probably best to treat these as annuals and purchase them new each year.

The popular water hyacinth produces waxy, vase-shaped leaves with swollen air-filled bases and orchidlike pale lavender flowers that stand about 4" (10 cm) above the water. The trailing roots provide excellent fish refuge.

Resembling a tiny water lily, frogbit has small heart-shaped leaves about 1" (2.5 cm) across and tiny, inconspicuous green flowers.

Water lettuce has velvety bluegreen foliage in the form of rosettes about 6" (15 cm) across. The trailing roots provide ideal fish habitat.

The water soldier has foliage resembling yucca. The spiky, dark olive green leaves may grow to 16" (41 cm) in height.

One native free-floating plant to consider is common duckweed (*Lemna minor*).

Common duckweed appears to have tiny leaves, but in fact these are part of a leaflike body that forms floating clusters. Its reproduction is so rapid that it can quickly form a green carpet over the entire surface of the pond. Pond maintenance will inevitably require periodic removal of part of this carpet. Fish, who love to eat duckweed, will help too.

Both deep-water and free-floating plants are fine choices for small container water gardens. On a sunny deck try planting the *Nymphaea* 'Comanche' water lily with a couple of water hyacinths in a 3' (91 cm) - deep, glazed, dark-colored ceramic pot with thick walls. The color will absorb heat, and the thick walls will retain it overnight. Even though the lily prefers deeper living arrangements, it will bloom splendidly, and if the water temperature is constant and warm enough, the water hyacinths with produce wonderful purple blooms. Throw in a little duckweed for texture.

Designing Small Container Water Gardens

Regardless of size, every pond must contain oxygenating plants to help establish ecological balance and impede the growth of algae. From there, you can consider any number of pleasing combinations, but be sure to include some deep-water and free-floating varieties and a few tall species to add vertical interest. Containers will restrict the growth of free-floating and deep-water plants, which can be prolific in larger ponds.

Here is a delightful combination for a small container on a deck or balcony. You will need a container with about 4–6 square feet (.4–.6 square meters) of surface area and about 2–3' (61–91 cm) of depth. A large terra cotta pot or half an old wooden barrel are about the right size for this miniature water garden.

To prevent seepage, barrels should be lined first with any of the quality liner materials available.

2 Parrot's feather (*Myriophyllum aquaticum*)
1 Swamp horsetail (*Equisetum fluviatile*)
1 Dwarf cattail (*Typha minima*)
1 Water lily (*Nymphaea 'Aurora'*)
3 Water lettuce (*Pistia stratiotes*)
1 Water hyacinth (*Eichhornia crassipes*)

As the parrot's feather begins to mature, its silvery-lime, feathery foliage will cascade over the pond edges. The many whorled branches of the swamp horsetail, borne on stalks up to 30" (76 cm) in height, will create an interesting transition between the soft, billowy foliage of the parrot's feather and the stark, bold 2' (61 cm) -tall stems of the

Even a small container can display free-floating, deep-water, emergent and submerged plants.

This low-maintenance water garden is easily filled and planted within a few hours. It will thrive in a sunny and warm location on a deck or patio.

dwarf cattail. The small water lily cultivar will add color to the pond with its olive green leaves mottled with reddish purple and its semi-double flowers that mature to a bright red-orange.

The floating foliage of the water lettuce and water hyacinth will complement the water lily nicely, and if conditions are ideal, the water hyacinth will display pale lavender blooms that will contrast the water lily blooms.

This miniature water oasis is ideal for close-up viewing throughout the summer. Two containers placed on either side of an entrance or conversation area can provide the sense of balance and repetition needed for a more formal space.

Designing Informal Ponds

A water garden in a casual setting should appear as if placed by nature, an effect achieved by establishing smooth transitional zones between various garden features. A pebble beach bordering a portion of a free-form pond, for example, will lead the eye naturally to the pond, especially if plants near the beach are complementary in form.

Here is a enchanting combination for a medium- to large-sized informal urban pond with approximately 100 square feet (9.3 square meters) of surface area.

BORDER AND EDGE

3 Hostas (*Hosta undulata* var. *albomarginata*)

3 Hostas *(Hosta fortunei* var. *aureomarginata)*

1 Hosta *(Hosta fortunei* var. *albopicta)*

5 Ostrich ferns *(Matteuccia struthiopteris)*

3 Maidenhair ferns *(Adiantum pedatum)*

5 Day lilies *(Hemerocallis fulva* 'Flore Plena')

3 Coral bells *(Heuchera* 'Palace Purple')

12 Bunny's tail grass *(Lagurus ovatus)*

3 Perennial flax *(Linum perenne)*

MARGINAL

3 Marsh marigolds *(Caltha palustris)*

EMERGENT

3 Arrowheads *(Sagittaria cuneata)*

5 Blue water irises *(Iris laevigata)*

5 Yellow water irises *(Iris pseudacorus)*

SUBMERGED (OXYGENATING)

5 Hornwort *(Ceratophyllum demersum)*

2 Canadian pondweed *(Elodea canadensis)*

DEEP-WATER

1 Water lily *(Nymphaea* 'Attraction')

1 Water lily *(Nymphaea laydekeri* 'Fulgens')

1 Water lily *(Nymphaea* 'Madame Wilfron Gonnère')

1 Water lily *(Nymphaea marliacea* 'Albida')

FREE-FLOATING

3 Frogbit *(Hydrocharis morsusranae)*

Even an old wooden canoe can become an interesting and unusual water feature.

The shallows and margins of the pond bordering the beach are interplanted with an array of contrasting forms and colors, including bold, coarse hostas, feathery ferns, sabrelike irises and tall, slender grasses. The green foliage will contrast with the yellow of irises and marsh marigolds. The warm colors continue into the water with a sequence of white, red and magenta water lilies.

Hornwort and Canadian pondweed, with their dense whorls of forked leaves, will supply oxygen to the pond and camouflage pumps, hoses and pots.

N. 'Attraction' is a hardy water lily with oval leaves that unfurl to a light bronze before turning dark green at maturity. The rich, deep garnet inner petals of the star-shaped flowers surround orange stamens. The young leaves of *N. laydekeri* 'Fulgens' have purple blotches and mature to deep green. Its semi-double burgundy-red flowers enclose orange stamens. From these deep reds, the lovely double pink blooms of *N.* 'Madame Wilfron Gonnère' provide an effective transition to the white of *N. marliacea* 'Albida.' All these lilies will spread 3–5' (1–1.5 m).

The free-floating frogbit completes the design with its lilylike heart-shaped leaves and tiny white flowers, and—if you're lucky—tiny white flowers.

Transplanting Water Lilies

Under typical prairie growing conditions water lilies become root-bound every two to three years and need to be repotted to maintain optimal flower production. Generally, it's best to transplant in the spring before the plants begin active growth.

When bloom production decreases, mature leaves are smaller than normal and yellow after only a few days, and leaves begin to pile up on one another, your lilies require repotting.

1 Fill a large, shallow container with heavy garden loam to about 1" (2.5 cm) from the top. Do not use commercial potting mixes because they typically contain vermiculite or perlite, both of which float, and do not use soil that has been amended with peat or other organic material. The addition of clay will make the soil more compact and stable. Mix a handful of bonemeal into the soil at the bottom of the pot to encourage root development

2 Soak the soil thoroughly with warm or hot water, and let it sit for one hour before planting.

3 Remove the pot from the pond to a shady location. Carefully remove the plant from its pot, and gently wash the soil from the rhizome. Rinse with clean water. Keep the plant damp throughout the process. If you are interrupted, leave it to float in water.

4 Prune out dead roots. Trim the long roots and the black end of the rhizome.

5 Prune out all old and damaged leaves, and separate and cut the growing tips, leaving approximately 2–6" (5–15 cm) of rhizome.

6 Place the rhizome at a 30° angle in the container, positioning the cut end near the container wall to provide maximum growing room for the other end. The crown (the growing point with young shoots) must remain above the level of soil and top dressing.

7 Firmly pack the mud around the rhizome.

8 If the soil is rich, fertilizing at this time is not essential. If desired, push three pond tabs or similar

fertilizer tablets into the soil for lilies, a process that should be repeated monthly until August Do not allow the tablets to directly contact the rhizome.

9 Top-dress the surface with .25" (.6 cm) of washed sand or 1" (2.5 cm) of washed pea gravel to protect plant crowns and prevent soil from washing into the pond and fouling the water. If you plan to stock your pond with fish, use only washed pea gravel to prevent them from dislodging the top-dressing.

10 Label a plastic stake with an indelible marker and insert it deeply into the pot.

11 Carefully lower the container to the proper depth in a location receiving at least six hours of direct sunlight. Use bricks to raise it if required.

The following water plants are available from many of the suppliers noted at the end of this book. Plants listed as hardy can generally be overwintered in the pond, provided that it does not freeze solid and plants are moved to deep water.

Tender plants can be overwintered indoors or, in some cases, treated as annuals.

Zone maps for the prairie provinces and states are found at the end of the plant list.

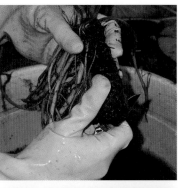

TRANSPLANTING A WATER LILY

1. After the soil is gently washed away from the roots, trim the dead portion of the rhizome.

2. Trim the roots to about 5" (10 cm).

3. If the rhizome has separate growing points, it can be divided into two plants.

4. Repot the rhizome with the freshly cut end against the container wall. Push the label deep into the soil.

COMMON NAME	BOTANICAL NAME	FLOWER DESCRIPTION	HEIGHT	SPREAD
Marginal				
Marsh reed grass	*Calamagrostis canadensis*	tiny, inconspicuous	24–48" (61–122 cm)	indefinite
Alpine marsh marigold	*Caltha leptosepala*	solitary silvery white	12" (30 cm)	12" (30 cm)
Yellow marsh marigold	*Caltha palustris*	bright yellow, 1–2" (2.5–5 cm) across	12" (30 cm)	18" (46 cm)
White marsh marigold	*Caltha palustris* var. *alba*	white	12" (30 cm)	18" (46 cm)
Double marsh marigold	*Caltha palustris* var. *plena*	double yellow, 1.5" (4 cm) across	12" (30 cm)	18" (46 cm)
Water sedge	*Carex aquatilis*	narrow brown spikes	24" (61 cm)	indefinite
Golden sedge	*Carex aurea*	brown, inconspicuous	15–36" (38–91 cm)	36" (91 cm)
Spike rush	*Eleocharis palustris*	.5" (1.25 cm) egg-shaped brown spikelets	12" (30 cm)	indefinite
Scouring rush	*Equisetum hyemale*	nonflowering	24" (61 cm)	indefinite
Siberian iris	*Iris sibirica*	dark-veined blue or blue purple	18–36" (46–91 cm)	indefinite

HARDINESS ZONE	BLOOM TIME	PLANTING CONDITIONS	COMMENTS
3	not applicable	boggy soil	produces seed heads in autumn
3	spring	boggy soil	heart-shaped dark green leaves
3	spring	boggy soil or up to 2" (5 cm) under water	poisonous; also known as cowslip, meadow-bright, kingcup, Mayblob
3	spring	boggy soil or up to 2" (5 cm) under water	poisonous; prone to mildew
3	spring	boggy soil or up to 2" (5 cm) under water	poisonous; often produces a second flush of blooms later in the summer
3	summer	boggy soil	a favorite food of wild and domestic animals, especially cattle and horses
5	summer	boggy soil or up to 2" (5 cm) under water	golden and yellow tufts of grassy foliage
3	summer	boggy soil or up to 2" (5 cm) under water	dense chivelike foliage with fine vertical texture
3	not applicable	wet, sandy bog soil	leafless stocks with bamboolike joints
3	late spring to early summer	boggy soil	also grow well in drier soil

COMMON NAME	BOTANICAL NAME	FLOWER DESCRIPTION	HEIGHT	SPREAD
Watercress	*Nasturtium officinale*	white	12" (30 cm)	indefinite
Palmate-leaved coltsfoot	*Petasites palmatus*	white	10" (25 cm)	4" (10 cm)
Arrow-leaved coltsfoot	*Petasites sagittatus*	white	12" (30 cm)	4" (10 cm)
Reed grass	*Phragmites australis*	purplish, dense and feathery	3–9' (1–3 m)	indefinite
Western dock	*Rumex occidentalis*	reddish, dense clusters	20–60" (51–152 cm)	8" (20 cm)
Pencil cattail	*Typha angustifolia*	brown spikes	5–7' (1.5–2.2 m)	3' (1 m)
Common cattail	*Typha latifolia*	beige spikes	8' (2.5 m)	indefinite
Dwarf cattail	*Typha minima*	rust brown spikes	18–24" (46–61 cm)	12" (30 cm)
Emergent				
Water Plantain	*Alisma plantago-aquatica*	white with pink hue	30" (76 cm)	18" (46 cm)
Water Hawthorne	*Aponogeton distachyos*	white	2–4" (5–10 cm)	4' (1.25 m)
Pink Flowering Rush	*Butomus umbellatus*	rose-pink	36" (91 cm)	indefinite

HARDINESS ZONE	BLOOM TIME	PLANTING CONDITIONS	COMMENTS
6	spring to early summer	shallow running water	peppery tasting leaves can be used in salads
3	early spring	moist soil at edge of pond	flowers appear before leaves form
3	early spring	moist soil at edge of pond	flowers appear before leaves form
3	autumn	moist soil at edge of pond	can be invasive
3	spring	boggy soil	common across prairies
3	autumn	plant 8–24" (20–60 cm) under water	decorative seed heads; can be invasive
3	late summer	plant 0–12" (0–30 cm) under water	can be invasive
6	late summer	plant 0–6" (0–15 cm) under water	decorative cylindrical seed heads
3	summer	plant up to 10" (25 cm) under water	native to prairies; also known as mad-dog weed
9	early spring, again in late autumn	plant up to 24" (61 cm) under water	may become dormant in summer heat; good in partial shade; vanilla-scented flowers
3	summer	plant up to 16" (41 cm) under water	propagate by division; do not plant in natural ponds

COMMON NAME	BOTANICAL NAME	FLOWER DESCRIPTION	HEIGHT	SPREAD
White water arum	*Calla palustris*	white spathe	10" (25 cm)	12" (30 cm)
Floating marsh marigold	*Caltha natans*	white-pink, .5" (1.25 cm) across	8" (20 cm)	indefinite
Stream horsetail	*Equisetum fluviatile*	spore clusters	24" (61 cm)	indefinite
Common scouring rush	*Equisetum hyemale*	spore clusters	36" (91 cm)	indefinite
Mare's tail	*Hippuris vulgaris*	tiny, inconspicuous	2–13" (5–33 cm)	12" (30 cm)
Japanese iris	*Iris kaempferi*	reddish purple to purple	24–36" (61–91 cm)	indefinite
Blue water iris	*Iris laevigata*	blue	30" (76 cm)	indefinite
Yellow water iris	*Iris pseudacorus*	yellow	48" (122 cm)	indefinite
Kermesina water iris	*Iris versicolor* var. 'Kermesina'	magenta	24" (61 cm)	indefinite
Parrot's feather	*Myriophyllum aquaticum*	tiny, inconspicuous	2–4" (5–10 cm)	indefinite
Water smartweed	*Polygonum amphibium*	pink	water's surface	indefinite
Broad-leaved pondweed	*Potamogeton natans*	inconspicuous	water's surface	indefinite

HARDINESS ZONE	BLOOM TIME	PLANTING CONDITIONS	COMMENTS
3	spring	plant up to 2" (5 cm) under water	produces red or orange berries
3	spring	plant up to 2" (5 cm) under water or in boggy soil	creeping; poisonous; less showy than *Caltha palustris*
2	nonflowering	plant up to 2" (5 cm) under water or in boggy soil	resembles asparagus fern
2	nonflowering	plant up to 2" (5 cm) under water	native to prairies; unusual jointed stems; can be invasive
3	late spring	plant 0–2" (0–5 cm) under water	native to prairies; can be invasive
3	early to midsummer	plant 0–2" (0–5 cm) under water	prefers partial shade
4	midsummer	plant up to 4" (10 cm) under water	also grows well in wet, boggy soil
4	midsummer	plant up to 4" (10 cm) under water	also known as yellow-flag or water-flag; prefers partial shade
2	summer	plant up to 2–3" (5–8 cm) under water	also grows well in wet, boggy soil
6	not applicable	plant up to 4" (10 cm) under water	bright green feathery stems form vines that will trail over pond sides
1	summer	0–4" (0–10 cm) under water	native to Alberta; does well in shallow water or moist soil
1	summer	0–4" (0–10 cm) under water	native to Alberta; showy bronze foliage

COMMON NAME	BOTANICAL NAME	FLOWER DESCRIPTION	HEIGHT	SPREAD
White water crow-foot	*Ranunculus aquatilis*	white	0–2" (0–5 cm)	indefinite
Yellow water crow-foot	*Ranunculus gmelinii*	yellow	0–2" (0–5 cm)	indefinite
Water soldier	*Stratiotes aloides*	inconspicuous	12" (30 cm)	indefinite
Arrowhead	*Sagittaria cuneata*	white	8–20" (20–51 cm)	indefinite
Water canna	*Thalia dealbata*	violet	5' (1.5 m)	24" (61 cm)
Wild rice	*Zizania aquatica*	pale green, grasslike	36" (91 cm)	not applicable
Deep-water				
Common white water lily	*Nymphaea* 'Alba'	white, semi-double	water's surface	5–6' (1.5–1.8 m)
Attraction	*Nymphaea* 'Attraction'	deep garnet inner petals, lighter outer petals	water's surface	4–5' (1.3–1.5 m)
Aurora	*Nymphaea* 'Aurora'	yellow-apricot, then red	water's surface	24–36" (61–91 cm)
Comanche	*Nymphaea* 'Comanche'	yellow-apricot, then orange-red	water's surface	4.5' (1.4 m)

HARDINESS ZONE	BLOOM TIME	PLANTING CONDITIONS	COMMENTS
2	summer	plant 0–24" (0–61 cm) under water	native to Alberta
3	summer	plant 0–24" (0–61 cm) under water	native to Alberta
6	late summer	floats on water's surface	treat as an annual in prairie ponds
3	summer	plant 0–4" (0–10 cm) under water	native to prairies; also known as wapato or swamp potato; also grows well in wet, boggy soil
6	summer	plant 0–6" (0–15 cm) under water	tubular flowers carried above leaves
2	summer	plant up to 9" (23 cm) under water	self-seeding annual
hardy	June to October	12–36" (30–91 cm) under water	best in medium to large ponds
hardy	June to October	15–36" (38–91 cm) under water	leaves open light bronze and turn dark green at maturity; best in larger ponds
hardy	June to October	12–18" (30–46 cm) under water	ideal for container garden or small pond
hardy	June to October	12–18" (30–46 cm) under water	leaves open bronze-green; good for medium to large ponds

COMMON NAME	BOTANICAL NAME	FLOWER DESCRIPTION	HEIGHT	SPREAD
Darwin (formerly Hollandia)	*Nymphaea* 'Darwin' *(formerly Nymphaea* 'Hollandia')	light pink inner petals, white outer petals	water's surface	4–5' (1.3–1.5 m)
Escarboucle	*Nymphaea* 'Escarboucle'	crimson tipped with white, semidouble	water's surface	4–5' (1.3–1.5 m)
Fabiola (formerly Mrs. Richmond)	*Nymphaea* 'Fabiola' *(formerly Nymphaea* 'Mrs. Richmond')	pinkish red with white	water's surface	5' (1.5 m)
Gloire du Temple-sur-Lot	*Nymphaea* 'Gloire du Temple-sur-Lot'	shell pink then white	water's surface	4–5' (1.3–1.5 m)
Gonnère	*Nymphaea* 'Gonnère'	white, double	water's surface	3–5' (1–1.5 m)
Laydekeri Fulgens	*Nymphaea laydekeri* 'Fulgens'	crimson-magenta	water's surface	3–5' (1–1.5 m)
Pink Gonnère	*Nymphaea* 'Madame Wilfron Gonnère'	light pink, double	water's surface	4' (1.3 m)
Chromatella	*Nymphaea marliaceae* 'Chromatella'	canary yellow, cupped shaped	water's surface	3' (1 m)
Marliac white	*Nymphaea marliacea* 'Albida'	white	water's surface	3–4' (1–1.3 m)
Perry's Baby Red	*Nymphaea* 'Perry's Baby Red'	deep red	water's surface	30" (76 cm)
Ray Davies	*Nymphaea* 'Ray Davies'	pink, double	water's surface	3–5' (1–1.5 m)

HARDINESS ZONE	BLOOM TIME	PLANTING CONDITIONS	COMMENTS
hardy	June to October	12–18" (30–46 cm) under water	best for medium to large ponds
hardy	June to October	12–18" (30–46 cm) under water	best for medium to large ponds; blooms late into afternoon
hardy	June to October	12–18" (30–46 cm) under water	best for medium to large ponds
hardy	June to October	12–18" (30–46 cm) under water	best in large ponds; large root system requires large container
hardy	June to October	12–18" (30–46 cm) under water	best for medium to large ponds; blooms late into afternoon; also known as crystal white or snowball
hardy	June to October	12–18" (30–46 cm) under water	one of the earliest blooming lilies; mottled brown leaves; good for any size pond
hardy	June to October	12–18" (30–46 cm) under water	best for medium to large ponds
hardy	June to October	12–18" (30–46 cm) under water	mottled bronze green leaves; good for any size pond
hardy	June to October	12–18" (30–46 cm) under water	produces large number of blooms for size; good for any size pond
hardy	June to October	8–12" (20–30 cm) under water	great for container gardens or small ponds
hardy	June to October	12–18" (30–46 cm) under water	good for medium ponds; flowers evenly colored

COMMON NAME	BOTANICAL NAME	FLOWER DESCRIPTION	HEIGHT	SPREAD
La Beaugère	*Nymphaea* 'Rene Gerard'	rosy red with white flecks	water's surface	5' (1.5 m)
Rose Arey	*Nymphaea* 'Rose Arey'	deep pink, double	water's surface	4–5' (1.3–1.5 m)
Sioux	*Nymphaea* 'Sioux'	orange-yellow to deep orange-red	water's surface	4' (1.3 m)
Texas Dawn	*Nymphaea* 'Texas Dawn'	yellow	flowers held well above water's surface	3–5' (1–1.5 m)
Virginalis	*Nymphaea* 'Virginalis'	pure white	water's surface	3–4' (1–1.3 m)
Virginia	*Nymphaea* 'Virginia'	cream to pale yellow	water's surface	5–6' (1.5–1.8 m)
William B. Shaw	*Nymphaea* 'William B. Shaw'	pink	flowers held just above water's surface	3–4' (1–1.3 m)
Red pygmy	*Nymphaea pygmaea* var. 'Rubra'	deep pink	water's surface	30" (76 cm)
Yellow pygmy	*Nymphaea* 'Helvola'	canary yellow, tiny	water's surface	24" (61 cm)
Yellow pond lily	*Nuphar variegatum*	yellow	water's surface	4–5' (1.3–1.5 m)

HARDINESS ZONE	BLOOM TIME	PLANTING CONDITIONS	COMMENTS
hardy	June to October	12–18" (30–46 cm) under water	good for medium to large ponds; leaves up to 1' (30 cm) across
hardy	June to October	14–24" (36–61 cm) under water	large root system requires large container; anise-scented blooms
hardy	June to October	3–4" (1–1.3 m) under water	good for medium to large ponds; blooms late into afternoon
hardy	June to October	12–18" (30–46 cm) under water	one of the best yellow flowering varieties; requires heat; good for any size pond; makes excellent cut flower
hardy	June to October	15–18" (38–46 cm) under water	good for any size pond; very free flowering in cool conditions
hardy	June to October	12–18" (30–46 cm) under water	best for medium to large ponds; distinctive star-shaped flowers
hardy	June to October	12–18" (30–46 cm) under water	good for small to medium ponds
hardy	June to October	6–18" (15–46 cm) under water	thrives in cool water; good for small container gardens
hardy	June to October	6–18" (15–46 cm) under water	dwarf variety; spotty brown leaves; flowers open in late afternoon; ideal for small, shallow ponds or containers
hardy	June to August	up to 12" (30 cm) under water	native to prairies; short blooming season; also known as spatterdock

COMMON NAME	BOTANICAL NAME	FLOWER DESCRIPTION	HEIGHT	SPREAD
Cape Cod	*Nymphaea odorata* var. *rosea*	pale to mid-pink	water's surface	4' (1.3 m)
Submerged				
Hornwort	*Ceratophyllum demersum*	indistinct	will rise near water's surface	indefinite
Canadian pondweed	*Elodea canadensis*	nonflowering	will rise to water's surface	indefinite
Common bladderwort	*Utricularia vulgaris*	yellow	water's surface	12" (30 cm)
Free-floating				
Fairy moss	*Azolla caroliniana*	nonflowering	water's surface	indefinite
Water hyacinth	*Eichhornia crassipes*	pale bluish lilac	8" (20 cm)	indefinite
Frogbit	*Hydrocharis morsus-ranae*	tiny, white	1" (2.5 cm)	indefinite
Common duckweed	*Lemna minor*	inconspicuous	water's surface	indefinite
Water lettuce	*Pistia stratiotes*	green, inconspicuous	6–12" (15–30 cm)	indefinite

HARDINESS ZONE	BLOOM TIME	PLANTING CONDITIONS	COMMENTS
hardy	June to October	12–24" (30–61 cm) under water	scented, star-shaped flowers; good for small to medium ponds
3	not applicable	24" (61 cm) under water	nonrooted; propagate by cuttings; also known as coontail
3	not applicable	1–7' (30 cm–2.2 m)	excellent oxygenator; does well in shade
5	summer	1–5' (30 cm–1.5 m) under water	can be grown in cold water aquarium; needs full sun
7	not applicable	floats on water's surface	quick growing; excellent autumn color; also known as mosquito plant
8	late summer	floats on water's surface	requires constant warm water temperature and full sun to bloom on prairies; interesting foliage; nearly impossible to overwinter on prairies
7	summer	may root in very shallow water near edge of pond	prefers still, shallow water
2	summer	floats on water's surface	native to Alberta; can be invasive; a favorite of water fowl and goldfish
8	late summer	floats on water's surface	treat as an annual in prairie ponds

Prairie Provinces Zone Map

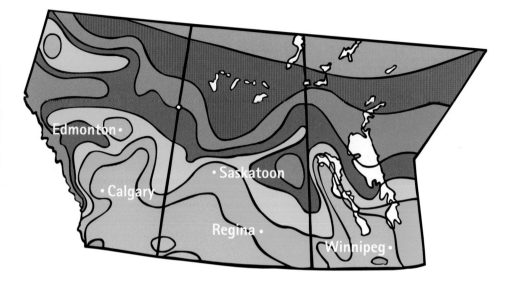

Average Annual Minimum Temperature

Temperature (°C)	Zone	Temperature(°F)
Below -55C	0a	Below -60F
	0b	
Below -45C	1a	Below-50F
	1b	
-45 to -42C	2a	-50 to -46F
-41 to -39C	2b	-45 to -40F
-39 to -37C	3a	-40 to -36F
-36.9 to -35C	3b	-35 to -30F

Prairie States Zone Map

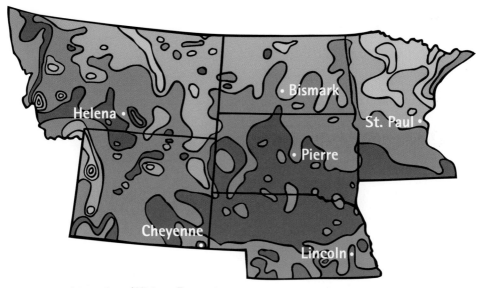

Average Annual Minimum Temperature

Temperature(°C)	Zone	Temperature(°F)
-42.8 to -45.5	2a	-45 to -50
-40.0 to -42.7	2b	-40 to -45
-37.3 to -40	3a	-35 to -40
-34.5 to -37.2	3b	-30 to -35
-31.7 to -34.4	4a	-25 to -30
-28.9 to -31.6	4b	-20 to -25
-26.2 to -28.8	5a	-15 to -20
-23.4 to -26.1	5b	-10 to -15

CHAPTER 4

Maintaining Water Gardens

ONE OF THE BEAUTIES OF THE water garden is the relatively little maintenance it requires once a balanced ecosystem is established. Beyond removing spent blooms and decaying leaves and applying the occasional fertilizer tablet, about the only routine maintenance throughout the gardening season is topping up the pond.

However, despite your best efforts, unsightly algae blooms frequently occur in newly planted ponds. Abundant sunlight acting on nutrient-rich water stimulates the rapid reproduction of these most basic of plants. Commercial algicides may be applied if no fish or plants are present, but it is preferable to let the pond establish a natural ecological balance. If conditions in the pond are right, this should occur within six to eight weeks after the pond has been aug-

The distinctive shape of common cattails is beautifully silhouetted against the setting sun.

99

A small pond vacuum operating off the pressure of a garden hose can be used to remove algae.

mented with natural pond water and oxygenating plants begin to compete for nutrients. Free-floating plants also will rob the algae of the plentiful sunlight needed for photosynthesis. To encourage a healthy balance, keep one-third to one-half of your pond covered with water lilies and floating aquatics such as water hyacinth, water lettuce, duckweed or frogbit. Remember, patience is a virtue. Every pond needs time to establish an ideal ecological balance. Be prepared to put up with an algae bloom or two.

To encourage submerged aquatic plants to take hold in a pond beleaguered with algae, temporarily raise them nearer the surface with bricks, where they can receive more sunlight. Once the water clears they can lowered to their proper depth.

Pesticides, weed killers and lawn fertilizers are all toxic in varying degrees to thriving pond life. The fine spray created by pesticide applicators can easily drift into the pond, killing fish. Weed killers interfere with plant photosynthesis. Lawn fertilizers add excessive nutrients, stimulating the production of algae and disrupting the pond's natural ecological balance. The best protection against the harmful effects of chemicals is not to use them, and if you must, then only under wind-free conditions well away from the water garden. Ensure that runoff from fertilized areas of the landscape cannot enter the pond.

If the pond shows symptoms of contamination such as recurrent algae blooms and dying fish, stop the source and take quick action to dilute the pollutant through a series of daily water exchanges. Ideally, you should not replace more than 10 percent of the pond's volume per day (an amount equal to 3–4" / 8–10 cm in a pond approximately 36" / 91 cm deep). If the problem is more serious, take more aggressive action by replacing up to 25 percent of the water daily, but expect an algae bloom to follow in two to three weeks. An activated charcoal filter added to your pump system may absorb some of the noxious chemicals, and running your waterfall or fountain round the clock will allow more oxygen to enter the water and more waste gases to exit.

Establishing a Natural Ecological Balance in Ponds

1 If possible use rainwater rather than chlorinated tap water to fill your pond.

2 When water temperature and quality allow, introduce three to five bunches of oxygenating plants for each square yard (meter) of surface area. Submerged aquatics like elodea, stonewort, mare's tail and common bladderwort are ideal for the prairie climate.

3 Provide shade for the pond by adding water lilies and free-floating plants.

4 Inoculate the pond with at least 4–5.5 U.S. gallons (15–21 l) of natural pond water rich in invertebrates. Collect the natural pond water close to shore, making certain it contains plenty of small water creatures.

5 After stocking the pond with fish, monitor the activity of small invertebrates. If their numbers appear to be in serious decline, add more natural pond water until the colony can sustain itself.

6 Do not overfeed fish. A well-balanced pond ecosystem will provide a large portion of the nutrients required by fish, so only light feedings every one or two days should be needed. Feed only as much high-protein fish food as can be consumed in three to five minutes. Surplus food should be scooped from the surface to prevent it from sinking to the bottom, where it will decompose and create an excessive supply of nutrients and possibly promote an algae bloom.

7 Run your fountain, stream or waterfall frequently to improve oxygen levels and release noxious gases that form from decomposing plant matter and fish waste.

8 Do not drain the pond for winter. The ice cover is a deterrent to liner damage, and a new ecosystem won't have to be established from scratch next season.

Maintaining Ponds Throughout the Seasons

SPRING

1 When spring has solidly taken hold and the risk of the pond freezing over has passed, remove the pond heater (if used to overwinter fish) or the insulating material (if used to overwinter

plants). If the straw bales used to overwinter aquatic plants are still in good condition tarp them over and save them for next fall. If not, compost them.

2 Using a skimming net, remove any leaves from the top of the leaf net, and then take out the net.

3 Reposition any construction materials from the pond edge and moving water feature that frost action has dislodged.

4 Using a skimming net or pond vacuum, remove any accumulated debris from the pond bottom. Very dark pond water with a foul smell is a sign of an overabundance of decomposing vegetation that will upset the pond's natural balance. Pump about two-thirds of the water onto your flower or vegetable garden. Then pump some into a holding tank, and remove aquatic plants and any fish. Empty the remaining water, and scoop out the decomposed material. Do not clean the walls so thoroughly that the bacteria coating on the pond walls and floor is removed. This bacteria is a passive filter that helps break down nutrients that nourish undesirable algae and result in unsightly blooms. Refill the pond with clean water and return approximately 4–5 U.S. gallons (15–19 l) of water from the holding tank. Add rocks to the pond bottom to encourage bacteria growth if algae blooms have been a problem.

5 Check electrical outlets and equipment for damage.

6 Top up the pond level, allowing chlorine to dissipate for several days before returning aquatic plant or animal life to the pond. If you have overwintered fish in the pond, it may be wise to let water stand for several days in a separate holding tank before adding it to the pond. At the same time add about 4–5 U.S. gallons (15–19 l) of natural pond water rich in organisms to help the pond quickly reestablish ecological balance.

7 Flush pumps, hoses and filters with clean water, and return them to the pond. Carefully check the operation of fountains, waterfalls, streams and biofilters.

8 Water lilies that have been overwintered indoors should not be returned to the pond until the temperature reaches 50°F (10°C).

9 If fish have been overwintered indoors, test the pond temperature before returning them to their summer home. It should be at least 59°F (15°C). Do not feed the fish until they are swimming actively.

10 Add new water plants as required.

SUMMER

1 Top up the pond as required. The typical evaporation rate of prairie ponds is about 2" (5 cm) per week,

but obviously above-average temperatures, high winds and fountain or waterfall action will increase water loss. Under normal conditions, a 2–3' (61–91 cm) - deep pond will need additional water every seven to ten days. Avoid adding more than 10 percent of the pond's volume at one time if you are using tap water.

2 Deadhead spent water lily blooms and remove yellowing leaves.

3 Add a fertilizer tablet to each water lily about once a month or more frequently if flowers or leaves are undersized or new growth has a yellowish cast.

4 Be diligent in removing any filamentous algae or debris that you find in the pond.

5 Free-floating plants such as frog-bit, duckweed and water hyacinth should be thinned if they become invasive. No more than 50 percent of the surface should be covered by vegetation.

6 Monitor water quality regularly in hot weather, especially if your pond is stocked with fish. If fish are routinely observed near the surface, they are not being friendly but are lacking oxygen. Run your waterfall or fountain more frequently to increase oxygen content or add a separate bubbler.

7 Clean the pump filter frequently. Setting the pump on bricks 2–4" (5–10 cm) from the bottom will help prevent clogging.

8 If a biofilter is used, flush it with pond water as required. Do not use tap water because the chlorine will kill the nitrifying bacteria.

9 Add a few inches of dampened peat moss to the bog garden as required to reduce moisture loss through evaporation.

AUTUMN

1 When water temperatures drop to 59°F (15°C), install a pond heater or move koi indoors. To help koi adjust quickly to the aquarium use pond water. If they are to remain in the pond, ensure that the heater will maintain a temperature of at least 59°F (15°C). As winter approaches, reduce the frequency of feedings and change from a high protein to high carbohydrate food, which is more easily digested by the sluggish fish. Their waste also will be less toxic under this feeding regime.

2 When water temperatures drop to 50°F (10°C), bring hardy water lilies and tender oxygenating plants indoors for overwintering. Remove large foliage, but don't disturb the tiny crown leaves. Place the plants in water-filled tubs and store them in a cool area. The ideal room temperature is 40–45°F (5–7°C). Do not allow the crowns to dry out, and top up the container occasionally with fresh water to prevent stagnation. Storing rhizomes in wet peat

Tender oxygenating plants and exotic lilies are removed from the pond for overwintering.

moss in plastic bags also works well and takes up less space. However, because the roots have been disturbed, they may take longer to reestablish themselves in the pond next season.

3 Remove floating aquatics and add them to the compost pile. Duckweed will form resting buds that sink to the bottom of the pond to overwinter, so leave them in place.

4 Divide and transplant bog plants as required.

5 Remove pumps, hoses, filters or other accessories that may be damaged by freezing. Do not drain the pond for winter. Leaving ecologically balanced water will give a head start to next year's garden.

6 Do not allow floating leaf debris to become waterlogged and sink to the bottom of the pond, where it will release methane gas and unwanted nutrients. If no insulating material will top the pond for the winter, add a leaf net.

7 With care, some hardy, marginal and oxygenating plants can be overwintered in the pond if it is prevented from freezing solid. Trim foliage and move deepwater plants to the deepest part of the pond, where the risk of freezing is reduced. Hardy marginals can remain in place on pond shelves. Place sturdy lumber over the pond, stack straw bales on top and then cover with a waterproof tarp.

WINTER

1 If you are overwintering fish in the pond, check the pond heater periodically. The pond heater will not generally keep the entire surface free of ice, but don't be tempted to chop holes because the shock waves can kill or stun the dormant fish. If you must remove some ice, melt it with boiling water.

2 If you are overwintering aquatic plants indoors, check them frequently. Always keep the crowns covered with water.

3 Winter is the time to pull a chair up to the fireplace and plan additions to your water garden. Check the suppliers' list at the back of this book, order some catalogues and plan for a water garden scene even more enjoyable than last year's.

Straw bales placed over timbers will allow you to overwinter many hardy species in the pond.

CHAPTER 5

Stocking Fish and Attracting Wildlife

A N ADDED BENEFIT OF YOUR water garden's beauty and tranquillity will be the diversity of wildlife it attracts. It seems only a matter of moments after filling your pond that creatures appear to give it nature's stamp of approval. Don't worry—every pond gets approved. After the addition of water, plants and animals, the pond will take several weeks to become ecologically stable. You will need to monitor the balance and perhaps adjust it from time to time, but beyond that, most of the work will be done by the plants and animals that reside in your pond.

Your pond provides four environments in which animals live: the surface of the water, the subsurface, the vegetation in and around the pond, and the bottom of the pond.

Six groups of wildlife will be

Brilliantly colored goldfish move serenely among lilies and irises.

107

Left: Mayflies will be attracted to your water garden.

Right: Damselflies, which consume mosquitoes, are welcome visitors to water gardens.

interested in making a home in or around your pond. They include microscopic animals, insects, aquatic animals such as fish and snails, amphibians, birds and mammals. Each has different accommodation requirements that you must satisfy if your pond is to be a wildlife haven.

For your efforts you will be rewarded with an ever-changing scene. Fish will glide gracefully among the water plants, feeding on aquatic insects. A toad or two may take up residence in the bog garden surrounding the pond. Iridescent dragonflies will hover in the air, and birds will visit to bathe and feed. Over time, your pond will become a miniature ecosystem.

Protozoa, bacteria, algae and fungi will form the plankton that is the bottom link of the food chain. Insect nymphs, larvae and pupae will feed on the plankton, and they in turn will feed fish and larger insects such as dragonflies, damselflies, pond striders and water boatmen. Amphibians and birds will prey on larger insects. A large pond in an ideal location may attract squirrels, rabbits, raccoons, muskrats and even deer.

Creating Special Habitats
FISH

The ideal water garden ecosystem should include fish. Though a number of native species are suitable, many gardeners are turning to exotic, decorative species such as goldfish and koi. Hardy goldfish varieties include common goldfish, comettails, fantails and black Chinese moors. Goldfish on a proper diet can reach lengths of 4–6" (10–15 cm) in about three years and require a pond depth of at least 2' (61 cm).

Koi, especially varieties such as higoi or nishikigoi, can grow to lengths in excess of 3' (91 cm) and

can live as long as seventy years. Koi need additional swimming space, so your pond must be at least 3' (91 cm) deep (and deeper if possible) and a minimum of 10–12' (3–3.7 m) in length. Even then, they may outgrow their environment.

The surface area of your pond is critical in determining the number of fish that can be safely stocked. As a general rule, the pond will require 2 square feet (.19 square meters) of surface area for every 1 linear inch (2.5 cm) of mature fish (less the tail). The formula assumes a pond depth of at least 2' (61 cm). Adding an another foot (31 cm) of depth will only marginally increase the pond's ability to sustain more fish. This guideline also assumes your pond has enough oxygenating plants to maintain a uniform ecological balance.

A pond 5' x 10' (1.5 x 3m) with a surface area of 50 square feet (4.65 square meters) will ideally support 25" of fish, or about 6 goldfish 4" (10 cm) in length or 2 koi 12" (31 cm) in length.

Above all, don't overstock your pond. The waste from too many fish will add additional nutrients, upsetting the ecological balance and raising the prospect of an algae bloom. Also, bear in mind that your fish will grow, so stock on the basis of mature size.

To calculate the surface area of your pond use the following formulas. For a rectangular pond simply multiply the length times the width. For a circular pond divide the diameter in half to yield the radius. Then square the radius and multiply by 3.14 (pi / π). For a pond with a diameter of 10' (3 m) the formula yields a surface area of 78.5 square feet:

10' (3m) ÷ 2 = 5' (1.5m) / 5' (1.5m) x 5' (1.5m) = 25 (2.25m) / 25 (2.25 m) x (π) (3.14) = 78.5 square feet (7 square meters).

The flashing colors of exotic koi add vibrancy and surprise to the water garden.

Koi can be trained to eat from your hand.

survive temperatures approaching freezing and as high as 84°F (29°C). Less hardy koi can survive temperatures as low as 59°F (15°C) and as high as 84°F (29°C).

Overwintering fish on the prairies presents a challenge. The only real options are moving the fish indoors or heating the pond. A 66-gallon (300-l) aquarium—3' x 3' x 2' (91 x 91 x 61 cm)—with an oxygen pump will sustain about eighteen 4–6" (10–15 cm) goldfish or about three to four koi. Beyond that, a koi in every bathtub is probably not an option.

Pond heaters are expensive to run, but the reward of being able to enjoy your fish in the winter is a strong incentive even if the colder temperature makes them lethargic. Set the heater to the minimum tolerable temperature for goldfish or koi and check it regularly. In particularly bitter temperatures, it may be necessary to insulate the pond. Place sturdy lumber across it, stack bales of straw on top and cover with a waterproof tarp.

For irregular shapes, divide the surface into approximate rectangles and circles and calculate the surface area of each. Add the areas together to compute total surface area.

Fish will not thrive in the daily temperature fluctuations typical of small, black-bottomed garden ponds. Short-term fluctuations should be reduced by providing a reasonable amount of shade under the pond's surface. Rock edging overhanging the pond will help, but you should add several lilies or other aquatic plants with large floating leaves to provide additional shade. Ideally, a relatively constant temperature of near 64°F (18°C) should be maintained.

As long as temperatures do not fluctuate rapidly, hardy goldfish can

SNAILS

In modest numbers, ramshorn snails (with spiraled circular shells) are beneficial scavengers, eating algae, decaying plant material and excess fish food. Ramshorn snails can be purchased from some gardening centers. As a general rule add one snail for each square foot (.09 square meters) of surface area. Native pond snails (with cone-

A resident frog is one of the great rewards of a well-planned water garden.

shaped shells) are also scavengers, but since they tend to turn their attention to succulent young water lilies or other tender foliage, they must be treated as pests. Examine pots and the undersides of new lilies for telltale gelatinous egg masses and wash them off before placing the plants in the pond. Goldfish will generally help to keep the pond snail population in check.

AMPHIBIANS

Amphibians are great friends of the garden. As tadpoles and larval salamanders, they help keep the pond free of waste, and as adults they provide natural insect control.

To colonize your pond you may need to collect toad or frog eggs in the spring. Frog eggs can be found anchored in masses to oxygenating plants in shallow slough water in early spring. Toad eggs are laid in ropelike strands and appear some-

what later in the season. You may have to be relatively vigilant in your search for eggs because they hatch only a week after being laid. Once a frog or toad colony is established in your pond, it should perpetuate itself.

An amphibian-friendly water garden must provide ready access to the pond, vegetation for shelter, and cool, dark places to live. The ideal amphibian environment will include a small, gently sloping sand or pebble beach, a bog garden with tall native plants and small caverns dug into the soil.

To make a perfect toad house, dig a 1' (30 cm) -deep hole with a ledge at about the 6" (15 cm) point. Add 1" (2.5 cm) of sand. Place a short section of drain pipe at an angle from ground level to the bottom of the pit. Set a roof of stone or wood on the ledge to produce a cavern and backfill, leaving only the entrance open.

Rural prairie ponds may attract many species of birds such as the beautiful yellow-headed black bird and the marsh wren.

A natural arrangement of rocks with good exposure to the sun will provide hiding places for amphibians, and the heat it retains may attract a friendly and beneficial garter snake.

Providing the conditions that encourage wildlife to take up residence in and around your pond brings the special satisfaction that the natural world is closer to your door. Making your pond wildlife-friendly entails avoiding the use of pesticides, herbicides and other toxins. Amphibians especially will absorb chemicals through their skin. You also should avoid releasing pet-store amphibians because they are usually not hardy in the prairie climate and may carry diseases that can infect local populations.

BIRDS

A pond is an irresistible attraction to birds. They will come to dine, drink and bathe, and if conditions are right they may even set up residence nearby. Birds prefer a reasonably private setting with few people and even fewer cats. If you own a cat, put a warning bell on its collar.

Birds appreciate shallow water for bathing. Consider leaving one end of your pond with only 1" (2.5 cm) of water depth. To encourage birds to establish a home, consider installing nest boxes near the pond.

MAMMALS

If you are in a rural setting, mammals such as muskrats and even deer may be attracted to your water feature. Because deer can do con-

siderable damage to preformed and flexible liners when they wade into the pond for a drink, you may have to consider fencing the area.

Small terrestrial creatures prefer a natural protective canopy no farther than 10' (3 m) from the pond. A few coniferous shrubs or even deciduous ornamentals near the pond won't cause excessive problems. Since the habitats of many small creatures are similar, group rock piles, toad houses, protective plantings and pond ramps. Adding artificial light to your pond will attract wildlife in the evenings and extend your enjoyment.

A well-balanced pond ecosystem and sheltering plants provide a perfect environment for cedar waxwings and squirrels.

Water Garden Resources

As water gardening becomes more popular, more and more local nurseries are carrying supplies such as pre-formed and flexible liners, pumps and fountains, along with plant material. Here are some specialized sources for plants, supplies and designs.

Canada

A Fleur D'eau Inc.
C.P. 120 6 Road 237
Stanbridge E. PQ
Canada J0J 2H0
Phone (514) 248-7008
Fax (514) 248-4623
E-mail fleurdo@acces-cible.net
Plants, liners, pumps, foun-
tains, fish

Aquatics & Co.
Box 455
Pickering, ON
Canada L1V 2R7
Phone (905) 668-5326
Fax (905) 668-4518
E-mail aquaticsco@aol.com
Plants

Bearberry Creek Water Gardens
RR 2 Sundre, AB
Canada T0M 0X0
Phone (403) 638-4231
Liners, pumps, fountains,
plants grown on site; special-
izes in hardy aquatics and
natives

Burns Water Gardens
RR 2 Van Luven Road
Baltimore, ON
Canada K0K 1C0
Phone (905) 372-2737
Fax (905) 372-1708
E-mail wtrgdn@eagle.ca
Plants, liners, pumps, fountains

Designer Gardens
Site 43, Box 13, RR 4
Calgary, AB
Canada T2M 4L4
Phone (403) 208-2890
Water garden design

Golden Acre Garden Senters Ltd.
620 Goddard Avenue NE
Calgary, AB
Canada T2K 5X3
Phone (403) 274-4286
Fax (403) 275-5615

Hawaiian Garden Centre & Nurs-
ery Ltd.
134 Lake Street
St. Catharines, ON
Canada L2R 5Y1
Phone (905) 684-1556
Fax (905) 988-5353
Plants, liners, pumps, fountains

Hillier Water Gardens
P.O. Box 662
Qualicum Beach, BC
Canada V9K 1T2
Phone (250) 752-6109
Fax (250) 752-1890
Plants, liners, pumps, fountains

Holes Greenhouses
101 Belrose Drive
St. Albert, AB
Canada T8M 1M9
Phone (403) 419-6808
Fax (403) 459-6042
Plants, liners, pumps, fountains

Johns Garden Centre
433 South Industrial Drive
Prince Albert, SK
Canada S6V 7L9
Phone (306) 764-8311
Fax (306) 922-8919
Plants, liners, accessories

The Lily Pool
3324 Pollock Road, RR 2
Keswick, ON
Canada L4P 3E9
Phone (905) 476-7574
Plants, liners, pumps, fountains

Moore Water Gardens
Box 70
Port Stanley, ON
Canada N5L 1J4
Phone (519) 782-4052
Plants, liners, pumps, fountains

Niagara Watergardens
5340 Highway 20 RR 2
St. Anns, ON
Canada L0R 1Y0
Phone (905) 386-6404
Fax (905) 386-7178
Plants

Parkland Nurseries
RR 2 Red Deer, AB
Canada T4N 5E2
Phone (403) 346-5613
Fax (403) 346-4443
Plants, liners, pumps, fountains

Parkside Gardens
251 Demetri Way
Salt Spring Island, BC
Canada V8K 1X3
Phone (250) 653-4917
Fax (250) 653-4918
Plants, damp-land irises

Picov's Water Garden & Fisheries
Centre
380 Kingston Road East
Ajax, ON
Canada L1S 4S7
Phone (800) 663-0300
Fax (905) 686-2183
Plants, liners, pumps, fountains, fish

Pond Perfect Landscapes
Box 659
Wembly, AB
Canada T0H 3S0
Phone/Fax (403) 766-3119
Liners, pumps, filters and accessories

Pond Liners
Box 55
Nestleton, ON
Canada L0B 1L0
Phone (905) 328-3973
Fax (905) 986-5865
Liners up to 1 acre (.4 hectares) in size

Reimer Waterscapes
RR 3, Box 34
Tillsonburg, ON
Canada N4G 4H3
Phone (519) 842-6049
Fax (519) 688-5459
Plants, liners, pumps, fountains, fish

Sunworks Home and Garden Inc.
4924 Ross Street
Red Deer, AB
Canada T4N 1X7
Phone (403) 341-3455
Fax (403) 341-5754
E-mail shop@sunworks.ab.ca
Website www.sunworks.ab.ca
Fountains, statuary, design, installation, plants, pumps, home decor

Toko Garden Design Ltd.
Box 67038, Northland Village PO
Calgary, AB
Canada T2L 2L2
Phone (403) 288-7780
Water garden design and installation

Water Arts Inc.
4158 Dundas Street West
Etobicoke, Ontario
Canada M8X 1X3
Phone (416) 239-5345
Fax (416) 237-1098
Plants, liners, pumps, fountains

Water Creations
461 Dupplin Road
Victoria, B.C.
Canada V8Z 1B8
Phone (800) 316-6637
Pumps, liners, fountains, supplies

United States
Dickson Brothers Inc.
204 North Galloway
Mesquite, TX USA 75149
Phone (800) 475-7867
Fax (214) 288-7536
All pond materials

Kellyco Water Garden Center
1085 Belle Avenue
Winter Springs, FL USA 32708-9697
Phone (800) 327-9697
All pond materials

Imperial Water Gardens
2213 E. St. Vrain
Colorado Springs, CO USA 80909
Phone (719) 636-3942
(719) 240-POND (7663)
Fax (719) 575-0589
Plants, liners, pumps, fountains

Koi Lagoon
2715 East Mulberry
Fort Collins, CO USA 80524
Phone (970) 484-9162
Plants, fish, filtration, supplies

Lilypons Water Gardens
P.O. Box 10
Buckeystown, MD USA 21717-0010
Phone (301) 874-5133
Toll free (800) 879-5459
Website www.lilypons.com
All pond materials

Lilypons Water Gardens
Box 1130
Thermal, CA USA 92274
Phone (619) 397-4258

Paradise Water Gardens
404 South Brandon
Seattle, WA USA 98108
Phone (206) 767-9776

Santa Barbara Water Gardens
P.O. Box 4353
Santa Barbara, CA USA 93140
Phone (805) 969-5129
All pond materials

Van Ness Water Gardens
2460 North Euclid
Upland, CA USA 91786
Phone (714) 982-2425
All pond materials

Waterford Gardens
74 East Allendale Road
Saddle River, NJ USA 07458
Phone (201) 327-0721
Fax (201) 327-0684
E-mail splash@waterfordgar-
dens.com
All pond materials

Windy Oaks
W. 377 – 510677 Betts Road
Eagle, WA USA 53119
Phone (414) 594-3033
E-mail windyoaks@corenet.net
Plants, fish, accessories, design

Magazines
Water Gardening Magazine
49 Boone Village
Zionsville, IN USA 46077
Phone (317) 769-3278
Fax (317) 769-3149

Internet Resources
www.icangarden.com/cata-
logue/aquatic
http://www.icangarden.com

Societies
International Water Lily Society
Box 104
Buckeystown, MD USA 21717
Phone (301) 874-5503
Website http://h2olily.com

Prairie Water Gardening Society
The Wet Thumb Journal
Box 1054
Saskatoon, SK
Canada S7K 3M4

Water Garden Club of British
Columbia
Attention: Ray Arnett or Matt Yale
Phone (604) 946-9934
Publishes newsletter, The Ripple

Index